And made a bonfire
Of the mainspring of national identities to melt
    the folk into one puddle
And the three seconds of the present moment
By massacring those wordy fellows whose memories were
    bigger than armies.

Where any nation starts awake
Books are the memory. And it's plain
Decay of libraries is like
Alzheimer's in the nation's brain.

And in my own day in my own land
I have heard the fiery whisper: 'We are here
To destroy the Book
To destroy the rooted stock of the Book and
The Book's perennial vintage, destroy it
Not with a hammer not with a sickle
And not exactly according to Mao who also
Drained the skull of adult and adolescent
To build a shining new society
With the empties----'

For this one's dreams and that one's acts,
For all who've failed or aged beyond
The reach of teachers, here are found
The inspiration and the facts.

As we all know and have heard all our lives
Just as we've heard that here.

Even the most misfitting child
Who's chanced upon the library's worth,
Sits with the genius of the Earth
And turns the key to the whole world.

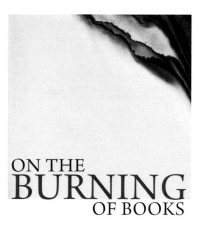

ON THE
BURNING
OF BOOKS

Dedicated to my book-loving grandchildren:
Tess, Oonagh, Conrad, Evie, Fraser, and Stanley

Published in 2016 by Unicorn,
an imprint of Unicorn Publishing Group LLP
101 Wardour Street, London W1F 0UG
www.unicornpress.org

ISBN 978-1-910787-11-3

Edited by Elisabeth Ingles
Picture research by Julia Brown and Benita Estevez
Index by Elizabeth Wise
Designed and typeset by Baseline Arts Ltd, Oxford
Printed in Slovenia for Latitude Press Ltd

ON THE
BURNING
OF BOOKS
Kenneth Baker

UNICORN

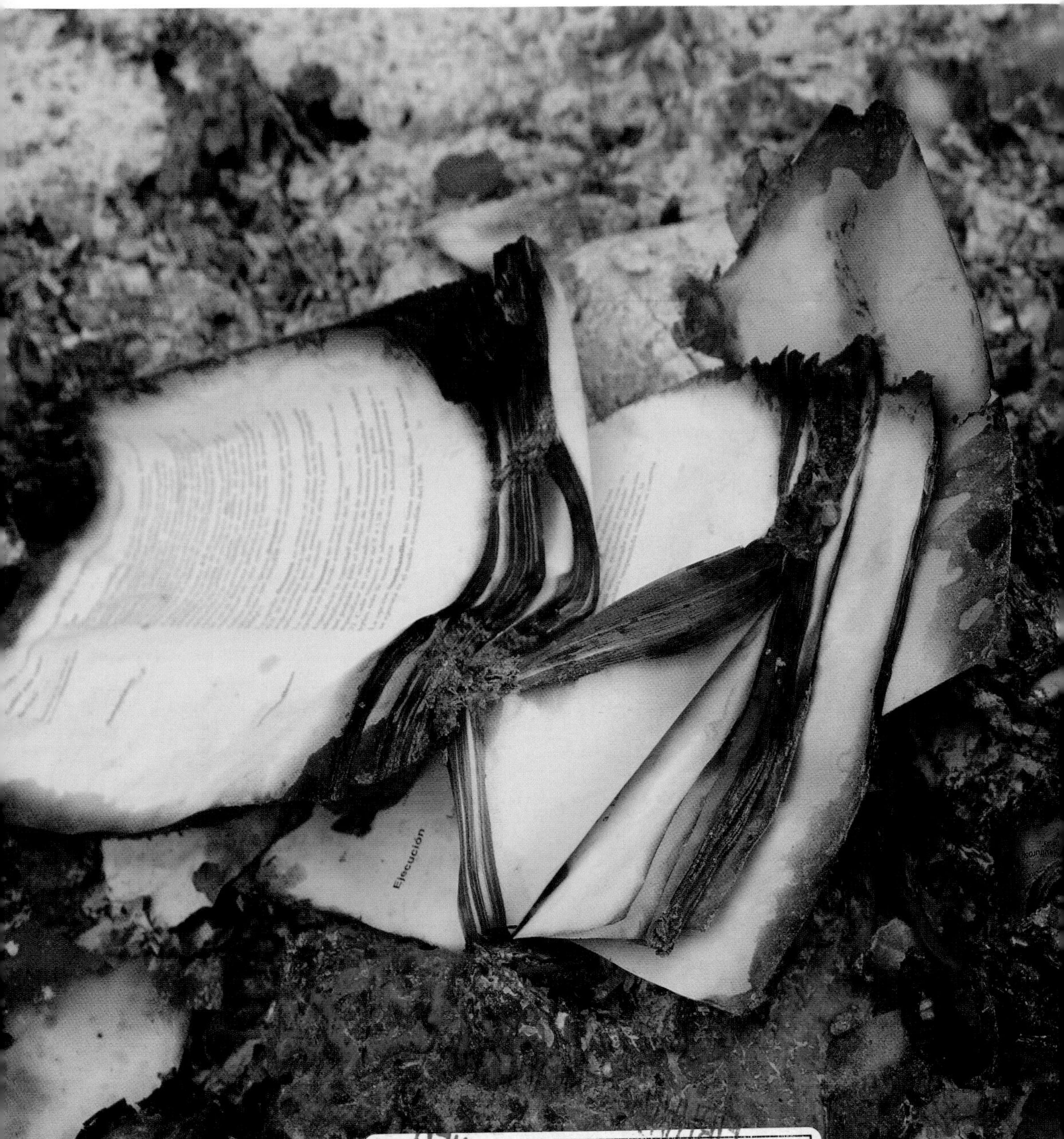
Ejecución

Contents

'The burning of a book is a
sad, sad sight, for even though
a book is nothing but ink
and paper, it feels as if the
ideas contained in the book
are disappearing as the pages
turn to ashes and the cover
and binding – which is the
term for the stitching and glue
that holds the pages together
– blacken and curl as the
flames do their wicked work.
When someone is burning
a book, they are showing
utter contempt for all of the
thinking that produced its
ideas, all of the labor that went
into its words and sentences,
and all of the trouble that
befell the author . . .'

Lemony Snicket
The Penultimate Peril

'The most characteristic activity
of the Nazis is burning books'
GEORGE ORWELL, 1941

Foreword

One of the books that I had to read in 1952 for the Higher School Certificate – which was to become the A Level – was Milton's *Areopagitica*. As I had never heard of it before, and as it had an uninviting Greek title and I hadn't studied Greek, and since it is a long essay, it didn't look as interesting as the other books we had to read: *King Lear*, *The Tempest*, *The Rape of the Lock*, *The Lyrical Ballads* and *The Woodlanders*. So I left it to the end. But I was soon enthralled by Milton's passionate and eloquent condemnation of censorship and his assertion of the right of every individual to think, write and speak freely – for that was to him the essence of personal and political freedom.

Milton's arguments were compelling but what made his great prose memorable for me was his eloquence in fashioning phrases and sentences that have resonated throughout history and are just as significant and relevant today:

'As good almost kill a man as kill a good book. Who kills a man kills a reasonable creature, God's image; but he who destroys a good book, kills reason itself, kills the image of God, as it were in the eye.'

'Give me the liberty to know, to utter, to argue freely according to conscience, above all liberties!'

'A good book is the precious life-blood of a master spirit, embalmed and treasured up on purpose to a life beyond life.'

'Books are not absolutely dead things, but do contain a potency of life in them to be as active as that soul was whose progeny they are; nay they do preserve as in a vial the purest efficacy and extraction of that living intellect that bred them.'

The lack of freedom of expression that rankled with Milton was Charles I's censorship of books and pamphlets, which led to their authors being pilloried or having their ears cut off or their noses split. He argued against the authority of the Star Chamber with its *Imprimaturs* – 'Let it be printed' – and its *Nihil Obstats* – 'Nothing stands in its way'. One of the many tragedies of Milton's life was that he was to see his words in *Areopagitica* ignored and even rejected by his friends. The Puritans of the Long Parliament were little better, for they banned all stage plays in 1642 and in 1644 they passed an Act to regulate printing; it was this that prompted Milton to write *Areopagitica*.

His hero, Oliver Cromwell, was just as censorious as Charles I. The Puritans smashed beautiful stained-glass windows, lamented by George Herbert in his poem *The Windows*, and they banned and burnt books as well.

To Milton the book was sacred, as it 'combined the memory of the past with a prospect of a life extending over centuries to come', and

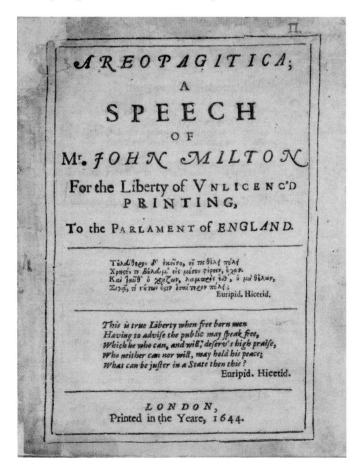

The title page of Areopagitica, *1644.*

this really started my long love affair with books. Their significance has been recognised in many civilisations throughout the world and throughout history. In the Abbasid Caliphate of the ninth century the great Arabic scholar Al Jahiz, born in Basra and writing mainly in Baghdad, observed:

'The composing of books is more effective than building in recording the accomplishments of the passing ages and centuries. For there is no doubt that construction eventually perishes and its traces disappear, while books handed down from one generation to another and from nation to nation remain ever renewed. Were it not for the wisdom garnered in books most of the wisdom would have been lost. The power of forgetfulness would have triumphed over the power of memory.'

In the twentieth century Jorge Luis Borges said, 'Of all men's instruments the most outstanding is, without any doubt, the book. The others are extensions of his body. The microscope, the telescope are extensions of his eyes; the telephone an extension of his voice, then we have the plough and the sword extensions of his arm: the book is extension of memory and imagination.' The key word is 'memory': for a book is not just a compendium of information, it also preserves the collective memory of its people with its foundation myths and fables, telling of its heroes and of battles won. It is the collective memory that any conqueror has to destroy. In Rome the Senate expunged the memory – *damnatio memoriae* – of those who had as traitors brought shame upon the city. George Orwell's totalitarian government in *1984* had a department whose duty it was to collect books on the written record of the past, to be burnt in secret furnaces. Ray Bradbury in his novel *Fahrenheit 451* (the temperature at which books burn) envisages a future America where all books are burnt, as they are old-fashioned, irrelevant or subversive. But there is a group of book drifters exiled to the country, where each learns a book by heart, so that the collective memory of America is preserved and one day they can be printed again.

Book burning has been so extensive and so perverse in its effect that I started to keep a note of the occurrences I came across –

which is how this book has come about. It does not attempt to be a comprehensive collection of all the many instances of man's folly – there are other studies that list all the libraries and collections, great and small, that have been destroyed and the individual volumes consigned to the flames. Such studies are usually written by scholars and librarians for scholars and librarians.

As books have been victims throughout history I decided to focus on those events where books have been burnt quite deliberately for political, religious or personal reasons, as the motive behind their destruction is what has interested me. It is a personal anthology.

One of the first things I discovered was that those who inspired or organised the destruction of books were not louts, looters or thugs, but well-educated people – often scholars who would have described themselves as civilised, just like the German professors who instructed their students to follow Goebbels's order to burn certain 'un-German' books. They all had a common characteristic – a conviction that their views must prevail, since theirs was the one certain route either to personal salvation or to political stability. If the retention of power, whether in a church, a mosque, a temple or a castle or cabinet room, was threatened by the written word, then throwing dangerous and offensive publications on the fire was the necessary first step to retain, enhance, defend and extend their power.

The power of religions or political regimes derives from their leaders' absolute conviction that what they are doing is right. It is this moral certainty that has driven so many religions and regimes to impose belief, to compel obedience, to censor and burn books, to spy on dissidents, to imprison, to torture and to kill. Totalitarian regimes – whether Fascist, Communist or Nationalist – and fanatics nurtured by fundamentalist religions become so convinced of the utter correctness of their own position that they can justify the burning, the elimination of dissidents and today the public beheading of prisoners. This certainty was behind the Inquisition in Spain, Calvin in Geneva, Stalin in Russia, Hitler in the Third Reich, Mao in China, the Stasi in East Germany, the Generals in Brazil and Argentina and today the Taliban, Al-Qaeda and ISIS.

The examples that I have collected fall broadly into three groups – political burning, religious burning and personal burning.

POLITICAL BURNING

Political leaders or dictators have used book burning to reinforce their control by intimidating their opponents, and to inspire their followers. The most well-known example in relatively recent history was the great bonfire organised by Goebbels in the Opernplatz, Berlin, on 10 May 1933. At midnight in his Fire Speech, he urged students to throw the works of Heinrich Mann, Stefan Zweig, and others (see p. 51) on to the flames of the bonfire, declaring that 'the era of Jewish intellectuals is over'. His first object was to use the fire as a means to cleanse and purify German culture, which he saw as having been polluted in the decadence of the Weimar period. In Hitler's own words the purpose was to obliterate an 'Un-German Spirit'. His second objective was to send a clear, visually memorable signal to the world that anyone who kept these works would be considered a traitor. Libraries were ransacked and even collections in private houses were seized, but he could never totally eliminate their books, as some were hidden under floorboards or in attics.

The bonfire in the Opernplatz, Berlin, 10 May 1933.

Many fires were also started across Germany, leading Orwell to remark, 'Book burning was the most characteristic activity of the Nazis.' But it didn't stop there, for the Nazis were about to fulfil the prophecy of Heinrich Heine in 1821, 'once they have burned books, they will end up burning human beings'. In the Holocaust the Nazis killed eleven million people, including six million Jews, at the extermination camps in Auschwitz and Treblinka in Poland, Janowska in the Ukraine, Maly Trostenets in Belarus and Sajmiste in Serbia, as well as many elsewhere.

In 1966 Mao Zedong launched his cultural revolution, ordering his Red Guards, clutching their *Little Red Books*, to organise bonfires across China to burn all writings that did not conform to Marxist-Leninist principles. He was determined to destroy China's traditional culture.

But the burning of books as a prelude to the more deliberate destruction of a culture did not just occur in the twentieth century. When Scipio Africanus finally defeated Hannibal at the Battle of Zama in 201 BC, the long-lasting Punic Wars were brought to an end. The Romans destroyed all the written records of Carthage, leaving it to Roman historians, especially Livy, to write the history – to the victors the laurels, in this case the obliteration of the past.

When the Spanish conquistadors discovered the Aztec culture in Mexico in 1519, they found they had stumbled upon a very sophisticated civilisation that had temples, great wealth manifested in gold and jade, books and rituals. After the initial pillaging of the gold, the Spanish set about destroying the entire civilisation, beginning with great bonfires of books, written records, pictures, idols and traditional ceremonial clothes. Great fires were held in 1530 and 1562 and eventually much of the Aztec culture was obliterated. Franciscan priests who led this campaign were scrupulous in keeping a record of manuscripts that were burnt, saving a few and sending them to the Vatican and Spanish libraries, which means that some of the best resources available for students of the Aztec civilisation are in European libraries.

It has become customary for revolutionary movements, which have used free speech to gain their ascendancy, to limit and even destroy that freedom of speech after they have triumphed. The censorship and suppression by Stalin was even greater than that by the tsars because it was more ruthless and efficient. Following the

Gorbachev liberalisation of the 1990s, President Putin, by his control of the press, television and radio, has all but eliminated free expression, even using the Stalinist weapons of show trials and assassination.

However, all these regimes contain the seeds of their ultimate collapse, for moral certainty alone is not enough to deal with the caravan of humanity. Whatever material benefits these regimes can offer, they will come up against the desire of a multitude of people to have the liberty to choose and the freedom to speak and to write whatever they want.

RELIGIOUS BURNING

Tacitus recorded that when the Romans reached Anglesey in the year AD60 they came across 'a circle of Druids lifting their hands to heaven and showering imprecations'. Rome showed no mercy and the priests of a foreign god were slaughtered. Most religions have persecuted non-believers, burning their books, destroying their places of worship and in many cases burning individuals at the stake or destroying them by other means.

For 600 years after the fall of the Roman Empire no heretic was burnt in Europe. The ruler who initiated this punishment was King Robert II of France, known as the Pious, when he ordered sixteen people to be burnt alive at Orléans in 1022, for these heretics denied the efficacy of baptism, the sanctity of marriage and the possibility of redemption from mortal sin; they also rejected the rank of bishops. From the first these trials were accompanied by brutal ferocity – a confessor of Robert's Queen, Constance, was one of the accused and as he left the court she poked out his eye with a wooden staff.

This burning created a sensation and spread across Europe in the eleventh, twelfth and thirteenth centuries. The First Crusade, proclaimed by Pope Innocent III in 1208 against the Albigensian heresy, was institutionalised savagery. When the town of Béziers was sacked and destroyed 20,000 people were put to the sword. When another crusader, Simon de Montfort, took the town of Bram he ordered the garrison to retreat with their noses cut off and their

The burning of the Jews in the war against heresy, woodcut, Nuremberg Chronicle, 1493.

eyes put out except for one man to lead them. What marked these centuries were brutal wars, torture and burning alive – all to preserve the Church of Rome – and in this case many records and traces of any distinctive language were consigned to the flame. It took a long time for burning to come to an end, for the last witch was burnt at Beaumont-en-Cambresis in northern France in 1835.

The Catholic Church was the first to create formally an Inquisition directed against the Cathars in France and later it established Inquisitions in Spain and Italy. Burning books by religions is a form of censorship enforced in the Middle Ages by torture and burning at the stake, and in later times by torture, arbitrary imprisonment, family harassment and the bullet. The development that stimulated the wrath of the Inquisition, but which was also to bring about its downfall, was the invention of the printing press. It has been estimated that in the whole of the fourteenth century clerical scribes across Europe produced a little over 2.5 million books. In 1550 the printing presses of Europe produced that number in just one year. This led Pope Paul IV in 1559 to establish the *Index of Forbidden Books* and to condemn anyone possessing any of these books or passing them to their friends. This could lead to an Inquisitorial investigation and in some cases death, but the task of policing it became too great, even for the Inquisition's bureaucracy. Pope Paul IV was a single-minded fanatic who never missed a meeting of the Congregation of the Inquisition, which took place every Thursday in Rome. The Inquisition was never popular and when he died a mob sacked its headquarters, torched its library and records and released its prisoners.

Considering the energy with which censors set about their work, it is astonishing how ineffective they have been. In 1526 Cuthbert Tunstall, the Bishop of London, discovered that copies of William Tyndale's translation of the Bible into English, which had been printed in the Netherlands, were circulating in London. He was so dismayed by this that his agents in the Netherlands tried to stop the Bibles being loaded on to ships. He then amassed all the copies he could find and

A printing shop in the Netherlands c. 1586. The spread of these shops all over Europe provided targets for the Inquisition and the Index of Forbidden Books, *but they also spelt the end of both institutions, as controlling the output of these presses became an impossible task.*

burnt them. Tyndale thought he was safe in the Netherlands but he was pursued by the Catholic Church and betrayed by a friend to the officers of the Holy Roman Emperor, Charles V, who had him burnt at the stake in 1536. His last words were, 'Ope the King of England's eyes.' That last wish was fulfilled by Henry VIII, who allowed English versions of the Bible to be used in his new Church of England shortly afterwards.

The Calvinists were no better than the Catholics and, inspired by John Calvin, they pursued and eventually captured Michael Servetus, a brilliant scholar and theologian who challenged the existence of the Trinity and the Calvinist doctrine of pre-destination in his book *The Restoration of Christianity*. He was sentenced, with the approval of Calvin, to be burnt at the stake with what was thought to be the last copy of his book. Calvin justified the burning of Servetus on the grounds that God had spoken and it was the duty of his servants to do whatever was necessary 'to combat for His glory'.

A contemporary example, in January 1989, was Salman Rushdie's *The Satanic Verses*, which was burnt in Bradford as a warning to authors not to attack the Prophet Mohammed. Rushdie had to flee and live under guard for ten years. The intimidation was ignored in England when Penguin and a group of publishers, to their great credit, agreed collectively to publish a paperback version. But overseas the bigots and the fanatics won out – in Italy Rushdie's Italian translator was beaten and stabbed; in Norway his publisher was shot; and in Turkey a mob burnt down the hotel where his interpreter was staying, which led to the deaths of thirty-seven people.

This is the twisted logic of fanatical bigotry and today it is echoed by other religions. Blasphemy laws are used in Pakistan to burn books and churches and to persecute Christians. Woe betide any writer or cartoonist anywhere in the world who disparages the Prophet Muhammad. The Jihadist terrorists who invaded the offices of *Charlie Hebdo* in Paris in 2015 shouted out 'Allahu Akbar' as they killed three cartoonists and nine other people.

PERSONAL BURNING

Many writers, as they come to the end of their lives, decide to edit the reputation they hope will survive them by destroying some of their remaining work, their letters and diaries, or instead leaving clear instructions to their executors or families to do just that. Byron's publisher John Murray decided to burn the poet's memoirs in the fireplace of his house in London. One of the most assiduous was Thomas Hardy, whose gardener saw him burning a vast amount of material including the early drafts of his poems and his notebooks, which were for him the source of many stories and characters; Lady Burton did the same for her husband's posthumous reputation; Mrs Kipling after her husband's death burnt a lot, including reputedly some anti-Semitic material; Philip Larkin asked his secretary and lover, Betty Mackereth, just before he died to shred his diaries; and E.M. Forster destroyed letters from his mother because over the years he had had a relationship with her which ranged from affection to disgust, but he did not destroy his twenty-eight diaries, including a 'locked one' which revealed many of his homosexual affairs. In his diary he noted, 'the older one grows the less one values security, perhaps anyhow I think there is little of me I feel was worthwhile to lock up'. When depositing their diaries some diarists insist that parts should not be available for a number of years, rather like Chips Channon MP, fearing that their diaries full of frank and acidic comments about their contemporaries would be seen as an assassin's cloak.

Some writers have sought to disown their earlier works. Borges admitted in his autobiography that he burnt his earlier books: 'About a few years ago if the price wasn't too high I would buy and burn them.' Graham Greene came to dislike his first book, a collection of poems, *Babbling April*, and later when he could get copies he destroyed them. Alexander Pope's first attempt at an epic poem was *Alcander*, which ran to 400 lines, but he burnt it. Gibbons's first attempt at history was *The History of Civil Liberty in Switzerland*, which he burned after it had met a cool reception from some of his friends. Both Tennyson and Browning took steps to cover their juvenile tracks. The motivation for personal burning varies, but it usually is a writer's search for privacy and discretion, rather than publicity and frankness.

In some cases destruction is driven by a search for perfection. Virgil asked his executors not to publish the *Aeneid* after his death, as there were several half-complete lines that he may have wished to finish, but the Emperor Augustus countermanded that request. Robert Herrick, the Cavalier poet, in true Virgilian fashion told his mistress in *His Request to Julia* to burn his poems if he died before they were printed:

> Better t'were my book were dead
> Than to live not perfected.

However, destroying a diary is almost tantamount to tearing up part of one's life, as Philip Roth noted: 'It takes more courage than one might imagine to destroy secret diaries…to obliterate forever the relic-like force of those things that almost alone of our possessions decisively answer the question: can it really be that I am like this?'

Instructions to executors can create difficult quandaries when they come to decide whether these should be followed – do the Dead have rights? Hardy's executors followed his instructions scrupulously but Max Brod, a close friend of Kafka who was told quite explicitly to destroy everything, refused to do so. This meant that the world has been able to read all Kafka's great novels, since they were printed after his death when he had envisaged that they would not be. Nabokov also gave instructions to his family to destroy everything, but his son decided to retain the fragments of his last novel, *Laura*, though when it was finally published most critics felt that Nabokov's request should have been followed. Authors were divided about this: Martin Amis and Tom Stoppard hated it while others such as John Banville considered it worth publishing.

It is appropriate that Hardy the committed burner should explain in a Hardyesque way the reasons why privacy and discretion, rather than disclosure and frankness, were to be desired: 'If all hearts were open and all desires known – as they would be if people showed their souls – how many gaspings, sighings, clenched fists, knotted brows, broad grins and red eyes should we see in the market place.'

Today the users of Twitter, Facebook and other social media have all done what Hardy feared and have experienced its fateful consequences.

Another chapter deals with burning as a result of war, where the destruction of books and libraries was not usually the purpose of the conflict – it was collateral damage. Millions of books have been lost through war, invasion and conquest, but I have included only a few examples.

A further chapter deals with accidental burning. Great calamities such as earthquakes, hurricanes, floods and lightning strikes have destroyed many libraries and books by accident. I have not attempted to catalogue all of these, concentrating only on the ones that seem to me to be remarkable. The eruption of Vesuvius destroyed the Villa of Calpurnius Piso, which contained one of the finest libraries of Greek and Roman books and manuscripts. The Japanese earthquake of 1923 flattened the Imperial University Library in Tokyo and a fire in Leningrad in 1988 destroyed 3.6 million volumes of the Soviet Academy of Science Library. On a rather lesser scale, the exquisitely bound copy of *The Rubàiyàt of Omar Khayyàm*, adorned with 1,050 precious stones set in gold, went down with the *Titanic*. Then there are the personal accidents, such as where a parlour maid uses a manuscript for fuel to start a fire.

A short chapter looks at royal burning, as several of our sovereigns have taken pains to remove material that they thought would be embarrassing.

The last chapter deals with lucky escapes, and some of these preserved really outstanding works of literature. But possibly the most famous of all was the rejection of Virgil's wish that the *Aeneid* should be destroyed as he had not finished it.

Books have many natural enemies: accidental fires or flooding, as water is just as damaging; and there are eighteen varieties of bookworm. The material on which the written word is recorded can decay or disintegrate – many of the Sumerian clay tablets have disappeared, broken up like clay pots; papyrus, which formed the libraries of Egypt and Greece, crumbles into dust if not properly looked after; and paper, particularly that treated by certain chemicals in the nineteenth century, decays. Vellum and parchment were sturdier and replaced papyrus, but they too had their enemies: in 1500 in the Jura some letters of St Jerome were lost when a bear ate them, attracted by the aroma of the parchment.

The first book to cover the destruction of books was published in 1880 by William Blades, a typographer and bibliophile: *The Enemies of Books*. It is a charming study of all the things that can harm books,

An American poster from 1942 quoting Roosevelt's words: 'Books cannot be killed by fire. People die, but books never die. No man and no force can put thought in a concentration camp forever. No man and no force can take from the world the books that embody man's eternal fight against tyranny. In this war, we know, books are weapons'.

but he singles out fire as being the most destructive: 'There are many of the forces of nature which tend to injure books; but among them all not one has been half so destructive as fire … chance conflagrations, fanatic incendiarism, judicial bonfires and even household stoves, time after time, have thinned the treasures as well as the rubbish of past ages.'

After Blades, words have been invented to describe the destruction of books – 'libricide' and 'bibliocide' – but they have found no place in common parlance and it is 'book burning' that sums it all up.

In the electronic age it is impossible to destroy information – the delete button does not delete; the material will turn up somewhere else. Today censorship is possible, as China has shown, but it is expensive, elaborate and almost certainly not comprehensive. So the burning of books has become technically unnecessary, but it survives as a symbol to impress the naïve, warn the dissenter and rally the faithful.

POLITICAL
BURNING

THE BURNING OF BOOKS IN CHINA

213BC

The great warrior Qin Shi Huang, having conquered seven states in the warring period (476–221BC), decided to unify them under the Qin dynasty, of which he declared himself the first Chinese Emperor. He was to become one of the great figures in the history of China. Qin started to build the Great Wall in the north and roads and canals to keep

Emperor Qin Shi Huang (220–210BC), 17th-century scroll.

his empire together. He standardised weights and measures, created a common currency and, most significantly, established a common script for the Chinese language. To ensure he was well protected in his afterlife he built a huge terracotta army complete with chariots, buried underground with him, which were discovered only in 1974.

Qin was a benevolent despot whose authority was imposed by his army, which suppressed any opposition. In 213BC he ordered that many old books were to be burnt, particularly the works of Confucius. Qin was determined to eliminate the collective memory, the history and traditions of his subject states and to suppress any political ideas or philosophical musings that would challenge his supremacy. The only books spared covered astrology, agriculture, medicine, divination and the history of the state of Qin.

In the warring period a Hundred Schools of Thought had flourished, but Qin closed these down and required absolute obedience to his own laws and decrees. He considered the Confucian philosophy, which encouraged the individual to follow a good example and become more independent, as dangerous. To encourage the burning of books he killed 460 scholars, probably by burying them alive – a slaughter that Mao Zedong admired, boasting that he had buried 46,000 scholars – 'We have surpassed Qin Shi Huang by a hundredfold'.

THE PEASANTS' REVOLT, JUNE 1381

The Revenge of the Unlettered

The Peasants' Revolt was England's first popular rebellion. In 1380 Parliament was bullied by John of Gaunt, whose recent expedition to France had been a disaster, to approve a poll tax of twelve pence per person, payable by every man and woman over fifteen, to meet the cost of more troops, a better fleet and the wages of soldiers in Calais, which were nine months in arrears. Each town or village was given a sum that they had to collect. As this was the third poll tax that had been levied, the king's government had created a highly effective machine to collect it. Local registers contained the details of what each person had to pay and these became the main targets of the mobs.

Labourers, artisans, cobblers, smiths, carters and farriers, usually led by parish priests, village notables and well-off farmers, were all determined not to pay and the first protests started in May 1381 in Essex and Kent villages. The houses of the collectors, the gentry and even abbeys were attacked and looted. In every case all the written documents that could be found were burnt by the rioters. In a village in Kent the sheriff was frogmarched to his own house where he was forced to surrender to the rebels fifteen rolls of the plan of the county and the royal writ announcing the tax. These were burnt by the rebel leader, Wat Tyler, in Canterbury.

The other leader was John Balle, a radical priest, who coined at a great meeting of 10,000 people at Blackheath the rebels' best slogan:

When Adam delved and Eve span
Who was then the gentleman?

When they reached London the rebels were joined by a great mass of Londoners, forcing the fourteen-year-old king, Richard II, to take refuge in the Tower of London with his leading ministers. On 14 June he agreed to meet the rebels at Mile End, since they were appealing to him above the barons and the great property magnates. He granted them all their demands including the abolition of serfdom and a fixed maximum rent of four pence an acre. The Archbishop of Canterbury, Sudbury, and the Treasurer, Hales, were left in the Tower, but a mob broke in and beheaded them and as Richard returned to central London he saw their heads on spikes at London Bridge.

This did not stop the looting – John of Gaunt's great Savoy Palace was razed to the ground; prison gates were broken down; and the Warden of the Marshalsea prison was beheaded. Richard once again agreed to meet the rebels in person at Smithfield; there he was greeted with a handshake by Wat Tyler, who repeated his terms – 'No Lordships. No outlaws. No serfs or villeins'. Nothing as radical as that had been heard before and was not to be heard again until the Levellers movement in the seventeenth century. Richard agreed to sign a document and to circulate the agreed policy, but one of his followers got into an argument with Wat Tyler and stabbed him to death. As Tyler's followers began to bend their bows to shoot at the royal party,

Richard, again very courageously, galloped straight up to the men and declared that he was their leader. They accepted this but time had been gained for the London militia to arrive and they began to herd the rebels out of London. The revolt was over.

The most distinguishing feature about this revolt was the number of bonfires started by the rebels, who hurled into them any documents they could find – manorial court rolls, rent rolls, records of feudal dues and outstanding fines, and the writs that announced the poll tax and recorded the amount due.

In St Albans the peasant farmers entered the abbey and, swearing an oath, reclaimed the ownership of the warrens, common roads and fields and asserted their right to hunt on the Abbot's lands. They burnt

This illuminated initial shows a freeman handing over the deeds to a property and receiving payment from another freeman. Only freemen were allowed to buy property – a source of anger and frustration among tenants.

in the marketplace the bonds that the farmers had had to surrender to the abbey for their good behaviour, together with the Archdeacon's manorial rolls and books relating to the Abbot's canonical jurisdiction. In Cambridge rebels forced the Master and scholars of the University to hand over all the charters, privileges and letters patent and these were all burnt in the marketplace, together with the University's archives. An old woman, Marjorie Starre, scattered the ashes into the wind, shouting, 'Away with the learning of clerks! Away with it.'

In July regal and local authority was restored: on 14 July John Balle was hanged and beheaded and 'his forequarters were sent to the four estates in the realm'. Richard II renounced all the agreements he had made and his revenge, and that of his supporters around the country, was savage – whenever any rebels were found they were beheaded on the spot.

The rebels believed that by burning written documents protecting the power and status of the wealthy there would be no written records of who owned what or how much was owed. Therefore only the collective memory of the common people could be relied upon. All written documents were seen as the weapons of a repressive state bearing down upon the unlettered peasantry – it was an assault upon the mechanics of officialdom and the whole structure of feudal obligations: 'The revenge of the unlettered'.

THE BONFIRE OF THE VANITIES

Bruciamente della Vanità, 1497

In April 1492 Lorenzo de' Medici, the great Renaissance Prince of Florence, deservedly called 'The Magnificent', was dying from a wasting fever at the relatively early age of forty-three in his villa outside the city. The mood of crisis seems to have been confirmed by unusual events: two caged lions mauled themselves to death and a thunderbolt hit the dome of the recently completed great cathedral. The doctor sent by his friend and ally, Ludovico 'Il Moro' Sforza, applied the traditional remedy for the rich – a potion of pearls and precious stones ground down – but it was to no avail. As death approached Lorenzo summoned to his bedside the ascetic, hook-nosed Dominican friar Fra Girolamo Savonarola to provide some comfort. But all he received was a lecture urging him to give up all his ill-gotten gains and return to the people their ancient liberties which as a tyrant he had ignored. However, Lorenzo's purpose was more to extract from Savonarola a pledge not to preach against his son, Piero, whom he knew to be a weak, vain playboy.

Lorenzo died the following day and was succeeded by 'Piero the Unfortunate'. The political power of the Medicis rested on their bank, whose most important client was the Papacy. Cosimo, the founder of the dynasty, and then Lorenzo had used their money to dominate the other Florentine families and make Florence, a relatively small state, a player at the top table of Italian politics – punching well above its weight. They were experts in the plots, intrigues, dynastic marriages and all the necessary political arts – bribery, corruption, torture and assassination. They also made Florence the cultural centre of the High Renaissance, using artists to foster their political fortunes – Lorenzo sent Botticelli to Rome to appease Sixtus IV, Leonardo da Vinci to Milan to win over the Sforzas; and they were quick to recognise the genius of Michelangelo.

It was for Piero a magnificent inheritance, but Florence's great wealth had created a society of extravagance, opulence and sexual indulgence. It was that which offended the ascetic Dominican Savonarola. He had been invited by Lorenzo to return to the monastery of San Marco, which was just a street away from the Medici Palazzo, and that became the centre for his campaign against the very things that made the city so great. His Lenten sermons from 1490 attracted huge attendances of 13,000–14,000 and he had trained his voice to carry through the cavernous aisles of the great churches and the cathedral. In these sermons he claimed to have visions from God and on one occasion to have had a conversation with the Virgin Mary. As a result he warned of the apocalypse that was to come unless all the gamblers, sodomites, prostitutes, blasphemers and bankers were driven out – bankers, in particular, because their sin was one of the gravest: usury. He urged his congregation to return to the early Christian virtue of self-denial.

Savonarola's prophecies of the doom that was to consume Florence and his sermons had a more political edge, predicting the fate that awaited tyrants who had abrogated the ancient liberties of the city and levied taxes on the poor to sustain their opulent grandeur. He had crossed the line from being a religious zealot to being a political prophet. When Charles VIII of France in 1494 decided to invade Italy to assert his claim to the kingdom of Naples, Piero denied him passage through Florence, but when a French supply army marched through Florence Piero fled.

After Piero vanished Florence was racked with battles between the various factions struggling for power, some supporting Savonarola and others wanting him to be driven out and killed. In this turbulent time his great triumph was his Lenten sermon in 1497, which urged all the people of the city to abandon their indulgent way of life and save

Contemporary portrait of Savonarola by his friend Fra Bartolomeo.

Savonarola preaching, woodcut.

their souls by giving up and discarding their vanities. The carnival that preceded Lent had become a riotous and lewd series of parties, much promoted by Lorenzo himself, who had composed his own bawdy ballads including 'We've all got cucumbers and long ones too'.

To check this Savonarola had been holding religious classes for young men and they now turned out in their thousands wearing white robes, singing hymns and going from house to house to collect the 'Vanities' – mirrors, statuettes, wigs (dead hair), dice, cards, gaming tables, splendid costumes and dresses, paintings, musical instruments, perfumes (lascivious odours), jewellery and lewd books – including Boccaccio's bawdy tales, Petrarch's love poems, Dante's poems and various works in Latin and Greek, including Ovid's *Ars amatoria*. They were all gathered in and taken to the Piazza della Signoria, where they were added to an enormous bonfire some sixty feet high with a circumference of 230 feet and seven tiers to remind everyone of the Seven Deadly Sins. The bonfire had so many valuable things in it that a Venetian merchant made an offer of 20,000 ducats for its entirety, which led to his effigy being added to the pile. On each tier there were sacks of straw, firewood, gunpowder and the vanities, all surmounted by an effigy of the devil. The fire was lit on 7 February 1497 to the accompaniment of a children's choir deriding luxurious living; trumpets sounded; bells pealed and the crowd roared.

This bonfire and his apocalyptic sermons had made Savonarola widely known across Europe: his thoughts and his revelations from God were published and read everywhere – nowhere more intently than in the Vatican. He had already predicted that the luxury and lasciviousness of the Church in Rome, where the Borgia Pope Alexander VI, allowed his children – Lucrezia and Cesare – to live in the Vatican, and the venal corruption of buying and selling bishoprics, would bring down upon Rome the fate of Babylon. Alexander VI was determined to silence Savonarola and asked the authorities in Florence to send him to Rome where he would certainly have been tried and executed, but that would have precipitated a riot in Florence. So, in May 1497 the Pope excommunicated Savonarola 'on the suspicion of heresy', which meant among other things that he could no longer preach. But he could not be silenced.

When Charles VIII abandoned his Italian ambitions the Pope made a deal with him and with the other powers in Italy that isolated

Savonarola's execution on the Piazza della Signoria in Florence (1498).

Florence. He planned a march on the city with the support of the Holy Roman Emperor and to intensify the pressure he threatened to put the whole city under an interdict so that no one could receive a Christian burial and therefore have no chance of going to heaven. The warring factions in Florence recognised that Savonarola was a liability and by that time many of its citizens had grown tired of his attempts to deny them their pleasures and pastimes.

The end was inevitable. His puritanical fanaticism made him almost a predecessor of Martin Luther, Oliver Cromwell, Robespierre and Lenin – he was quite as dangerous to the established regime as any of these. So the government of Florence had him arrested and handed him over to the Church to be tried. After being repeatedly tortured he made a confession that was to lead to a heretic's death of being burnt in the very square where the bonfire of the vanities had been held a year earlier. Two of his friars were burnt alongside him – each was hanged from a gibbet and left choking to death over the fire lit below them so that the flames would burn their flesh before they died.

Savonarola's fight was against a corrupt Church and a people that had given themselves up to an easy life of indulgent consumerism. He was not advocating a change to democracy, but he wanted people to accept a better way of life and he allowed no compromises. It was the classic conflict between fundamentalism and materialism – the very same conflict that has run throughout history and is so relevant at the present time – though the religious fundamentalism that is exerting its power today is Muslim, rather than Christian.

BEN JONSON (1572–1637)

The Isle of Dogs, 1597

The Isle of Dogs, written by Ben Jonson and Thomas Nashe, was performed by a group of actors known as Pembroke's men at the Swan Theatre on Bankside in July 1597. No text of the play has survived, but Jonson had blundered into the world of Elizabethan political satire for on 10 August a complaint about the play was referred to no less important a body than the Privy Council. Nashe fled to Great Yarmouth just before his lodgings were raided, but the authors must have been busy destroying any copies they may have had, for nothing was found there.

Jonson was arrested and imprisoned at the Marshalsea where on 15 August he was questioned by the key political figures of England – the Lord Treasurer, Cecil, the Lord Chamberlain, the Lord Chancellor, the Controller of the Household and the Chancellor of the Exchequer – and accused of 'lewd and mutinous behaviour', for

A contemporary drawing of the Swan Theatre, built in 1596 and the home of Pembroke's Men where The Isle of Dogs *was performed. It looks small but it could 'seat 3,000 persons' and so many must have seen the play.*

the play contained 'very seditious and scurrilous matter'. He was lucky to be released on 8 October. The nature of the offence is mere speculation, but at that time the Earl of Essex's plans to replace the Cecils were maturing and the play may have seemed to favour Essex.

As a Catholic Jonson was frequently in trouble with the authorities. In 1598 he had killed a man over a religious dispute and escaped death only by claiming 'benefit of clergy', though he was punished by being branded with a hot iron on the fleshy part of his thumb with the letter 'M' – manslayer. In 1605, after collaborating

Ben Jonson *by Abraham van Blyenberch.*

with Marston and Chapman on *Eastward Ho* – which included some jokes at the expense of Scottish courtiers – he spent two months in jail. By 1610 he had been adopted by the establishment and was charged to write the script for a magnificent martial show designed by Inigo Jones for Twelfth Night to celebrate the formal debut of the fifteen-year-old eldest son of the King, Prince Henry. Again in 1611 Jonson wrote for a similar occasion *Oberon, the Fairy Prince*.

Jonson was a master of social satire. After two essays into politics he veered to the right and became in the Civil War a champion of the Cavaliers; he was appointed Royal Laureate. Edward Hyde, the future Lord Clarendon, who was exiled in Holland with Charles II, recalled how 'the virtu and the example' of Jonson and his friends helped him to overcome his youthful degeneracy. He also thought that Jonson was 'the best judge of and fittest to prescribe the rules of poetry and poets, of any man who had lived with or before him'.

In 1597 the offending play could not be burnt since no copy could be found, but the authorities did not give up. On 1 June 1599 the Archbishop of Canterbury, John Whitgift, in his capacity as Chief Censor, and Bancroft, the Bishop of London, decreed that 'no satires and epigrams be printed hereafter and that all earlier ones should be burnt by Thomas Nashe, John Marston, Joseph Hall and Dr Harvei's boekes' – this led to the Bishops' Bonfire when all these books 'thereupon were burnte' at Stationers' Hall. Christopher Marlowe's translation of Ovid's *Amores* was added to the fire.

Jonson's View on Burning

One can never know how many plays were burnt, because so many have simply disappeared. Between 1560 and 1642 some 3,000 plays were written and performed, but only around 500 have survived. Political censorship clearly rankled with Jonson and he found a way to express his contempt for it in his play *Sejanus – His Fall*, 1603. Cordus is an historian in the time of the Emperor Tiberius who, writing about the assassination of Julius Caesar seventy years earlier, praised Brutus and Cassius, and this was interpreted by the Senate as possibly condoning an attempt on Tiberius' life. So the Senate decreed that Cordus' books were to be 'all sort out and burnt today'. Jonson's opinion of this was expressed by two senators:

Arruntius: Let 'em be burnt! Oh how ridiculous
Appears the Senate's brainless diligence,
Who think they can, with present power extinguish
The memory of all succeeding times.'

Sabinus: 'Tis true: when contrary, the punishment
Of wit doth make the authority increase
Nor do they aught, that use this cruelty
Of interdiction and this rage of burning
But purchase to themselves rebuke and shame
And to the writers an eternal name.'

For such frankness Sejanus has Sabinus killed and Arruntius is forced to commit suicide.

The Burning of Jonson's Personal Library, 1623

In 1623, the year when Shakespeare's *First Folio* was published, Ben Jonson suffered a great loss when his own library was accidentally burnt. The cause was unknown, but Aubrey in his *Brief Lives* hinted that it might have happened one night for 'he would many times exceed in drinke' and 'would tumble home to bed and when he had thoroughly perspired, then to studie. I have seen his studying chaire, which was of straw'. Perhaps a candle burnt down and fell over. Jonson was desolate and wrote a long poem, *An Execration upon Vulcan*. He was angry at the loss and how quickly the fire spread:

Thy greedy flame thus to devour
So many my years' labour in an hour.

Jonson also recorded in his poem some of the books that he had borrowed from fellow writers, his working papers and records:

All the old Venusine in poetry,
And lighted by the Stagirite, could spy
Was there made English, with a Grammar too,
To teach some that their nurses could not do,
The purity of language. And, among

The rest, my journey into Scotland sung,
With all th'adventures; three books not afraid
To speak the fate of the Sicilian maid
To our own ladies and in story there
Of our fifth Henry, eight of his nine year;
Wherein was oil, beside the succour spent
Which noble Carew, Cotton, Selden lent:
And twice-twelve years' stored up humanity,
With humble gleanings in divinity
Among the fathers and those wiser guides
Whom faction had not drawn to study sides.

The reference in the first line is to Horace who was born in Venusia and in the second to Aristotle who was born in Stagiria. His own account of a visit to Scotland, some story about Henry V and, most poignant of all, his commonplace book in which he had been recording interesting passages for over twenty-four years, were all lost. I suspect it was a fire that just consumed the papers on and around his desk, for if it had spread more widely it would certainly have burnt his house down, though he ascribes no blame to himself.

JOHN MARSTON (1576–1634)

John Marston, after graduating from Brasenose College, Oxford, in 1595, was enrolled by his father, a distinguished lawyer, into the Middle Temple. He soon started to write plays and entertainments for his fellow students, which led his father in his will to complain of his son's 'delights in plays, vain studies and tomfooleries'. His first printed work in 1598 was *The Metamorphosis of Pygmalion's Image*, published alongside 'certain satires'. These, together with the longer *Scourge of Villaine*, were imitations of Juvenal, full of moral outrage. Somewhat surprisingly for someone new to the scene of satire, these were added to the list to be burnt by the common hangman in 1599. In the same year Marston's father died, leaving him relatively well off, which allowed him to pursue his interest in play-writing. His most celebrated play, *The Malcontent*, appeared in 1604, targeting the evil men who abandon the Christian way of life. In 1609 he took holy orders 'and lived out his days in a disguise of quietude'.

JOHN MILTON (1608–1674)

Up to 1641 the thirty-three-year-old John Milton had published only poems, in both English and Latin, for his command of Latin was as fluent as his English and later it was to earn him the diplomatic post of Secretary for Foreign Tongues under Oliver Cromwell. Up to that time he had not been known for his radical views.

The Long Parliament, summoned reluctantly by Charles I in 1640, changed everything. In 1641 it abolished the Court of Star Chamber, which was the instrument Charles and Archbishop Laud had used to censor all manner of publications and to punish the authors. With the Star Chamber out of the way, a torrent of pamphlets flooded London that was eventually to wash the King away – between 1641 and 1645, 10,000 titles were published, 8,000 of them in revolutionary London.

In May 1641 Milton's first pamphlet, *Of Reformation Touching Church Discipline in England*, was an onslaught on the Bishops – 'vessels of perdition' destined for hell, where they would be treated with 'bestial tyranny'. Two others quickly followed and in 1643 he published a pamphlet that was to gain him notoriety, for it advocated divorce: *The Doctrine and Discipline of Divorce*. Divorce, for Milton, was a means of giving men greater freedom – he was no feminist and was an enemy of sexual profligacy. He was soon being denounced as 'The Divorcer' and one young divine, Herbert Palmer, denounced his tracts in a sermon to Parliament: 'A wicked book is abroad and uncensored though deserving to be burnt'.

In 1642 the Puritans of the Long Parliament passed a law that closed all theatres and banned plays from being staged 'to avert the wrath of God. Whereas publike sports doe not well agree with publike Calamities, nor publike Stage-plays with the Seasons of Humiliation, this being an Exercise of sad and pious Solemnity and the other being Spectacles of Pleasure, to commonly express lascivious Mirth

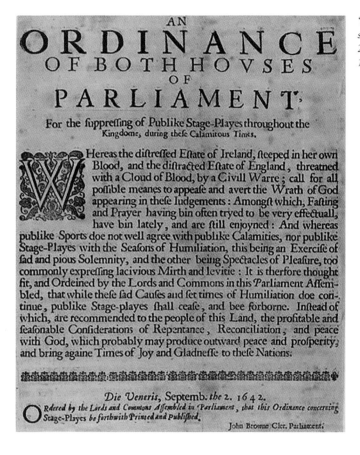

and Levitie'... and accordingly 'publike Stage-plays shall cease'. This infamous Ordinance led to the closure of the Globe Theatre in London and its demolition in 1644 by the landowner, Sir Matthew Brend, in order to build tenement houses.

An Act to regulate printing re-introduced licensing in much the same way as Charles I and Archbishop Laud had done. Milton was personally targeted by a stationers' petition against his tracts and the address where he lived was made public to allow personal protest. It was this that provoked Milton to publish *Areopagitica, for the Liberty of Unlicensed Printing* as 'a speech of John Milton' and in order to protect the printer and publisher from persecution or closure he omitted their names from the title page. This pamphlet was an act of defiance, followed up a year later with a poem expressing his anger *On The New Forces of Conscious* which ended with the all too accurate and damning couplet:

When they shall read this clearly in your charge
New Presbyter is but Old Priest writ large.

The trial of King Charles in January 1649 galvanised Milton into polemic action. A few days before the court trying the King came to its verdict he published *The Tenure of Kings and Magistrates*, justifying the overthrow and execution of a tyrant. Within a few months he got his reward when the Council of State that replaced the Crown appointed him as Secretary for Foreign Tongues – he took the revolutionary shilling. The Council asked him to reply to the famous pamphlet allegedly written by King Charles, *Eikon Basilike* ('The King's Image'), and in October 1649 *Eikonoklastes* ('The Image Destroyer') was published on the streets of London. This vicious political attack upon the King was followed by another in 1651, *Pro Populo Anglicano Defensio* ('A Defence of the English People'), which became a European bestseller and which Cardinal Mazarin in France ordered to be burnt in Paris and Toulouse. It was followed in 1654 by *Pro Populo Anglicano Defensio Secunda* – a propaganda diatribe praising Cromwell, who had just dissolved Parliament and set himself up as the Lord Protector of the Commonwealth of England, Scotland and Ireland.

Over the following three years Cromwell established a totalitarian regime where free speech was restricted; the press censored; newspapers closed down; and he appointed major-generals rather than Members of Parliament to rule the country. The very liberty that Milton had so eloquently advocated was suppressed and extinguished. Cromwell even personally ordered the burning of a satirical book written in 1655 by Milton's eldest nephew, John Philips, entitled *A New Spring of Lusty Drollery, Jovial Fancies and a la Mode Lampoons on some Heroic Persons of These Late Times*, on the grounds that they were 'scandalous, lascivious, scurrilous and profane'. So much for *Areopagitica*.

Milton was able to reconcile his devotion to Oliver Cromwell with his earlier views on the liberty of speech and the liberty of the press by regarding the execution of Charles I as part of God's will to save the Protestant nation. This was not face-saving, for to Milton and for many of those living at the same time, religion was the immediate,

John Milton,
engraving by
I. B. Cipriani,
London 1760.

central and supreme issue in the Civil War and the formation of
the republican government. For a long time it was fashionable to
diminish the religious convictions of both sides in the Civil War and
a Marxist interpretation gained ground, but, more recently, no doubt
reflecting the recognition of religion as the source of violent divisions,
the Miltonic preoccupation is more widely understood.

On 3 September 1658 Oliver Cromwell died and, when the
inadequacy of his son became apparent, General Monck, the
republican general, marched down from Scotland, intent on restoring
the monarchy.

Milton was appalled at the prospect of a Stuart restoration and
published a series of pamphlets extolling republicanism and the
toleration of religious beliefs: *Defence of the English People; Of Civil
Power in Ecclesiastical Causes Showing That it Is Not Lawful for Any
Power on Earth to Compel in Matters of Religion* – 16 February 1659;

Considerations Touching the Likeliest Means to Remove Hirelings Out of the Church – August 1659; *Readie and Easie Way to Establish a Free Commonwealth* – 1660, which advocated a commonwealth rather than a monarchy; and *Brief Notes upon a Late Sermon* – 1660, which promoted General Monck as the country's ruler rather than Charles Stuart. Milton was clearly aligning himself against the return of monarchy. This was dangerous stuff.

King Charles II entered London in triumph on 29 May 1660, putting an end to England's experiment with republicanism. Milton went into hiding, for he was not covered by the general amnesty proclaimed by Charles II and the proceedings for his arrest began in June – on the same day his books were removed from the Bodleian. On 13 August 1660 a proclamation was declared against *The Defence of the English People* and *Eikonoklastes*: both books by Milton were to be called in and burnt. On 27 August 1660 Milton's other books were publicly burned by the hangman at the Old Bailey. The restored monarchy had forgotten Milton's great line from *Areopagitica*: 'as good almost kill a Man as kill a good Book'. He had warned against spilling 'that seasoned life of man preserved and stored up in books: since we see a kind of homicide may be thus committed, sometimes a martyrdom and if it extend to the whole impression a kind of massacre'.

Two days after the book burning, the Act of Free and General Pardon, Indemnity and Oblivion was given Royal Assent. Milton, then fifty-two years old, blind and a social and political outcast, was not on the list of those sentenced to death but that did not save him from being imprisoned for two months. It was said that Charles II's view of Milton was 'he is old and blind and full of fleas, let him be'. So *Paradise Lost* was saved. Even after he had published that and *Paradise Regained* he was regarded as a dangerous radical republican. In Oxford on 21 July 1683 his books were 'publicly burnt by the hand of our Marshal in the court of our schools'. Many turned out in their full academic dress to witness this massacre of words and 'scholars of all degrees and qualities in the mean time surrounding the fire, gave several hums whilst they were burning'. A black day for this centre of civilisation.

SOLEMNE LEAGUE AND COVENANT

1661

Parliament in the sixteenth and seventeenth centuries could on occasion show its disapproval of a book or a political instrument by ordering it to be burnt by the public hangman. A former Librarian of the House of Lords Library, David Jones, estimated that between 1660 and 1710 there were about twenty cases when this happened.

One of the most significant of these occurred following the restoration of the monarchy in 1660. Both Houses of Parliament in May 1661 ordered that the Solemne League and Covenant be burnt in the new Pallace (sic) of Westminster, in Cheapside and before the Old Exchange on 22 May. This was the treaty approved by Parliament that John Pym had made with the Scots in 1643 when the Civil War was running against the Parliamentarians. The Scots promised to send an army of 20,000 men to fight against the King, as long as Parliament would introduce compulsory Presbyterianism in England and Wales – the Episcopacy and the Church of England would be abolished. The Scots Presbyters wanted this as a protection against any attacks upon their ascendancy in Scotland.

After the Royalist forces had been defeated, Charles I in 1647 was asked to support the Solemne League, which he refused to do. He knew that some of the Parliamentarians did not want Presbyterianism imposed, for it smacked of intolerance, and some looked upon it as almost as bad as the intolerance of the Episcopacy. Indeed, had not Milton written, 'New Presbyter is but Old Priest writ large'.

This allowed Charles to play for time, but he was not clever enough to steer a course through the various strands of republicanism and eventually his stubbornness led to his execution. Clearly for Charles II's government – which reinforced the power, status and privilege of the Church of England by denying dissenters any role in its public life – the Solemne League had to be consigned to the flames.

In 1667, when Clarendon, Charles I's first and most loyal leading minister and one of the great Parliamentarians of the Civil War, was in effect dismissed, he wrote a defence of his conduct, but both Houses declared that 'The humble Petition and Address of Edward

Earl of Clarendon… (voted to be scandalous and seditious; and that it doth reproach the King and the Public Justice of the Nation) shall be burned by the Hand of the Hangman … at the Gate of Gresham Colledge in Bishopsgate Streete in London on Thursday the Twelfth Day of this Instant December, between the Hours of Twelve and One of the Clock the same Day.' The concept of a Leader of the Opposition did not really exist in the seventeenth century but it was assumed that when a leading politician was dismissed he was dangerous and the book burning became a symbolic act of the new government, often a prelude to exile.

The other papers burnt by order of the two Houses were not so significant, but all seemed to be described as 'scandalous and seditious'. In June 1685 the Declaration of the Duke of Monmouth, in which he had announced his rebellion against James II, was burnt, as was a book in 1693 entitled *King William and Queen Mary Conquerors*.

JOHN WILKES (1725–1797)

Issue 45 of *The North Briton*, 23 April 1763

The Treaty of Paris which had ended the Seven Years War in 1763 was a triumph for Britain: France lost Canada and all her lands east of the Mississippi, and all her stations in India but four, though two sugar islands which Britain had conquered, Martinique and Guadeloupe, were returned to France. This was not good enough for John Wilkes, who denounced the Treaty in an anti-ministerial polemic in Issue 45 of *The North Briton* when he specifically condemned George III for his support of it, saying:

> 'every friend of his country must lament that a Prince of so many great and amiable qualities, whom England truly reveres, can be brought to give the sanction of his sacred name to the most odious measures and the most unjustifiable public declarations from a throne ever-renowned for truth, honour and unsullied virtue… I wish as much as any man in the Kingdom to see the honour of the Crown maintained in a manner truly bearing Royalty. I lament to see it sink, even to prostitution.'

The ministry decided to prosecute Wilkes for seditious libel and proceeded under a general warrant, which meant that virtually anyone could be arrested who had been involved in the publication, printing, writing or preparation of the pamphlet. In effect the ministry closed the paper by imprisoning its entire staff, even if no prosecution were to follow. Wilkes was imprisoned in the Tower, but Chief Justice Pratt in the Court of Common Pleas decreed that since libel was not a breach of the peace Wilkes as an MP was entitled to the privilege

Caricature of John Wilkes holding the cap of Liberty. By William Hogarth, 1763 Etching and engraving.

of Parliament and should be discharged – *Habeas Corpus* had triumphed. But Parliament rounded on Wilkes and decided that Issue 45 was libellous and ordered it to be burnt by the common hangman. The motion was passed by both Houses in spite of an eloquent intervention by its former leader, William Pitt the Elder.

The common hangman in setting fire to Issue 45 at the Royal Exchange managed to burn only a part of it, which allowed a mob of 500 to rescue the rest, pelt the sheriff and city marshal with mud and smash the glass of the coach of the sheriff, Thomas Harley MP. In spite of 200 constables being present no action was taken against the mob, which raised the cry that was to become famous, 'Wilkes and Liberty'. The King was outraged when the magistrates did not read the Riot Act, looking upon their inaction as amounting to connivance. There are two contemporary accounts:

A Letter from William Temple to James Boswell, then Living in Holland, on 23 November 1763

> We are all in a combustion here. Mr Wilkes has been wounded in a duel by Mr Martin of the Treasury. It was occasioned by some reflections in *The North Briton* and some words that passed in the House of Commons. Mr Wilkes is better. No. 45 is voted a false, scandalous and seditious libel and is to be burnt by the hands of the hangman.

Friday 9 December 1763, Horace Walpole to the Earl of Hungerford

> *The North Briton* was ordered to be burned by the hangman at Cheapside on Saturday last. The mob rose; the greatest mob says Mr Sheriff Blunt, that he has known in forty years. They were armed with that most bloody instrument, the mud-out-of-the-kennels; they hissed in the most murderous manner; broke Mr Sheriff Harley's coach-glass in the most frangant manner; scratched his forehead so that he is forced to wear a little patch in the most becoming manner; and obliged the hangman to burn the paper with a link, though faggots were prepared to execute it in a more solemn manner.

The burning had the reverse effect from that which the government intended. It made Wilkes a national hero and although he had to flee to France for a short time he returned to lead the opposition to George III's prime ministers for over three years with an avalanche of ridicule. His actions were a critical and significant stage in the development of a free press in Britain.

THE AMERICAN WAR OF INDEPENDENCE

Samuel Loudon (1727–1813): New York, 1776

Samuel Loudon was a merchant printer who ran a successful bookshop in New York in the 1770s. He was sympathetic to the rebels and the Sons of Liberty who were protesting at the overbearing and tax-levying government of George III in London, and so he started up a newspaper in January 1776 called the *New York Packet* to support 'our present much distressed country'. When the British occupied New York later in 1776 he fled to Fishkill and continued to publish the *Packet* from there until the end of the war. On 10 January 1776 Tom Paine's pamphlet, *Common Sense*, an eloquent plea for separation – 'It is time to part' – was published in Philadelphia and rapidly became America's first bestseller with over 100,000 copies being snatched up.

As the Continental Congress, a gathering of the thirteen States, did not at that moment in time seek independence, Loudon printed a pamphlet critical of *Common Sense* entitled *The Deceiver unmasked; or, Loyalty and Interest united*. The more radical leaders in New York did not like this scrupulous approach to a political dispute where the other side was allowed to state its case and on the night of 19 March a mob invaded Loudon's office and burnt the entire edition of 1,500 copies on the common. Loudon may even have been tarred and feathered, which was a punishment invented by the rebels in America to put pressure upon any officials or public figures sympathetic to the colonial government. However, he was forgiven and later in the year was given £200 to keep the *Packet* going.

Jemmy Rivington, New York Gazetteer

The colonial government's case did not go by default. Jemmy Rivington was the editor of the *New York Gazetteer*, which had the largest circulation in the colonies – 3,600 subscribers in October 1774. He dubbed the Whig newspaper, *The Boston Gazette*, 'Monday's Dung Barge' and *The Massachusetts Spy* that 'Snake of Sedition'. A mob hanged him in effigy on 13 April 1775 at New Brunswick and in reply

Loyalist officials and supporters of George III's colonial government were often tarred and feathered.

he published this image of himself being hanged for the defence of the free press. This was too much and early in May a mob attacked his house and printery and he had to seek safety on a British ship. Later another marauding party took away all his lead type. There was no room for dissent in the land of the brave and the free.

CONSEQUENCES OF A SUCCESSFUL FRENCH INVASION

James Gillray, 1 March 1798

A Cartoonist's Forecast of What Might Happen

James Gillray was the genius of the Golden Age of British cartooning from 1780 to 1830 – he spared no one. His targets were King George III, his profligate son the Prince of Wales and his brothers, the Prime Ministers Lord North, William Pitt and Lord Addington,

James Gillray, Consequences of a successful French invasion.

Consequences of a Successfull French Invasion.___N.º.I. Plate.1.st "We come to recover your long lost Liberties."Scene.TheHouse of Commons.

and the Leader of the Opposition, the Whig Charles James Fox. But Gillray was so appalled by the violence of the French Revolution and the consequences of its radical ideas spreading to England that he produced four prints envisaging the horrors that would ensue from a successful French invasion. In this print the Members of the House of Commons are manacled and dressed as convicts about to be despatched to Botany Bay; the Prime Minister, Pitt, and his friend, Dundas, are padlocked together; the Speaker is being manacled by two French soldiers while a drumstick has been stuffed in his mouth to prevent him from speaking out; a blacksmith with a hammer is breaking the Mace of Parliament, which symbolises its authority, into pieces; and a cobbler, wearing a cap of Liberty, is using bellows on a fire – called a Chaffer – which is consuming the journals and records of the House of Commons, thus destroying the history and authority of democracy. In addition there are branding irons in the fire, which would be used to scar one cheek of the Members before they set off for Botany Bay.

Fortunately for Britain, Napoleon's intended invasions of 1803 and 1804 were never launched. We were saved a revolution and a dictatorship.

AGE OF REASON

George Cruikshank, 1820: Another Cartoonist's Forecast

In the years 1819 and 1820 Britain came close to a radical upheaval or even revolution. There was widespread unrest, for since the victory at Waterloo in 1815 there had been a series of bad harvests leading to food riots across the country; the victorious soldiers did not find it easy to find employment at home; there were rick-burnings and raids on the new factories to break up the machines that were replacing labourers.

The reactionary Home Secretary, Lord Addington, maintained a network of spies across the country reporting on radical meetings, particularly in London and Birmingham. On 16 August 1819 the Manchester Yeomanry charged, with sabres raised, into a massed crowd at St Peter's Fields in Manchester that was being addressed by the radical orator Hunt, killing eleven people and injuring 400 – it became known as the Peterloo Massacre. Shelley wrote his famous sonnet, 'England in 1819':

An old, mad, blind, despised and dying king, –
Princes, the dregs of their dull race, who flow
Through public scorn, – mud from a muddy spring, –
Rulers who neither see, nor feel, nor know,
But leech-like to their fainting country cling,
Till they drop, blind in blood, without a blow, –
A people starved and stabbed in the untilled field, –
An army, which liberticide and prey
Makes as a two-edged sword to all who wield, –
Golden and sanguine laws which tempt and slay;
Religion Christless, Godless – a book sealed;
A Senate, – Time's worst statute unrepealed, –
Are graves, from which a glorious Phantom may
Burst, to illumine our tempestuous day.

The government was so alarmed that it introduced the Six Acts, which restricted the freedom of the press, banned meetings of over fifty people unless approved by a magistrate and introduced sweeping powers to search houses and seize weapons – the spirit of revolution was in the air.

The old king, George III, who had been confined to Windsor Castle for over ten years in a state of senile decline, died in January 1820. He was succeeded by his spendthrift, libertine son, the Prince Regent, who had been a target of the most scandalous caricatures.

In February 1820 a group of conspirators led by Arthur Thistlewood planned to blow up the Prime Minister, Lord Liverpool, and his Cabinet. Known as the Cato Street conspiracy, it was only frustrated by a report from a spy who had infiltrated the group. Five of the conspirators were hanged and five were transported to Australia.

The second six months of 1820 were dominated by the attempts of George IV to divorce his wife, Caroline. During the course of the trial, the scandalous life which she had led was laid bare and at the same time everyone was reminded of the many mistresses that George had maintained and the extravagant life he had led.

This print by George Cruikshank, the leading cartoonist of the day, envisages a revolution taking place. The Church is overthrown, bishops and politicians are hanged, the throne is toppled, the guillotines are prepared and the ardent supporters of Tom Paine are ready to launch an attack upon the Christian government, King and Parliament. Britannia lies stabbed and the laws of England, Magna Carta, the Bill of Rights, together with the Bible and the Prayer Book, are hurled into the flames. On the left those who have suffered persecution in the past – a Jew, a Negro, a Chinaman and an Indian – do not conceal their delight.

The Age of Reason, *George Cruikshank, 1820.*

THE SHELLS CRISIS

May 1915

The Burning of the *Daily Mail* and *The Times*

On Friday 14 May 1915 *The Times* carried a striking despatch from its military correspondent in France which reported, 'the want of an unlimited supply of high explosives was a fatal bar to our success' in the attacks along the Fromelles-Richebourg line. On the following Monday Lord Northcliffe, who owned both *The Times* and the *Daily Mail*, wrote an article himself under the headline 'The Shells Scandal', blaming Lord Kitchener, the Commander-in-Chief, for it:

> 'The broad facts of the matter are that Lord Kitchener, remembering the Boer War, pinning his faith to shrapnel and despite the urgent and repeated requests from our soldiers in France, did not realise until quite lately that the type of shell demanded by the present war is the high-explosive shell.'

Northcliffe then went on to praise the '*Manchester Guardian*, the foremost liberal journal in the North of England', which had also called for Kitchener's resignation:

> 'It is impossible that Lord Kitchener should escape responsibility and the chief responsibility for this failure.'

The Cabinet was thrown into a crisis which was to lead to the Conservative Party joining a new coalition government and Lloyd George being appointed Minister for Munitions. Nonetheless, many were appalled by Northcliffe's assault on someone who had been a national hero. The *Daily Mail* and *The Times* were burnt on the floor of the London Stock Exchange and the committee of the Manchester Stock Exchange passed a resolution that, 'in view of the disgraceful and unpatriotic attacks on those responsible for the conduct of the war no copy of *The Times* or the *Daily Mail* be allowed on the Manchester Stock Exchange'. Kitchener survived, but his ministerial colleagues continued to find him difficult. This was resolved by his death in July

1916 when, on a diplomatic mission to Russia, his ship HMS *Hampshire* was sunk by a mine. This calamity was greeted thus by C.P. Scott of the *Manchester Guardian,* 'as for that old man he could not have done better than to have gone down, as he was a great impediment lately'. Northcliffe's fierce patriotism had Kitchener and Asquith in his sights and he led a campaign for Lloyd George to take over as Prime Minister, which happened in 1916. Northcliffe was given the job as Head of the War Mission to the United States and then as Head of Propaganda in Enemy Territories, which earned him this German medal showing him sharpening his pen to dip into 'propaganda ink'.

The German Medal of Northcliffe.

THE SHELLS SCANDAL.

LORD KITCHENER'S TRAGIC BLUNDER.

OUR TERRIBLE CASUALTY LISTS.

CAUSE OF THE CABINET CRISIS.

The two things that have precipitated the Cabinet crisis are the quarrel between Lord Fisher and Mr. Winston Churchill and the revelation of a serious shortage of high-explosive shells.

Of these the second question, by far the more important of the two, was forced upon public attention by the military correspondent of *The Times* in a striking despatch from the front which was published last Friday. It was there stated specifically that "the want of an unlimited supply of high explosives was a fatal bar to our success" in the attacks along the Fromelles-Richebourg line.

This sentence, coming from such a source and published with the knowledge and consent of the Military Censors both in France and in London, attracted universal notice. It brought to a head misgivings that had long been forming in the public mind as to our supplies of ammunition. Questions were immediately asked in the House of Commons, but in view of the political situation were not pressed home.

The facts disclosed would have brought about the fall of the Government had not the Unionist leaders agreed to form a Coalition Ministry.

CONFIDENCE IN LORD KITCHENER.

RESOLUTIONS PASSED IN THE NORTH.

The following reply from Lord Kitchener to the resolution of confidence in him passed by members of the London Stock Exchange was received yesterday by Mr. C. C. Clarke, the proposer, and was posted in the Stock Exchange :—" Please accept for yourself and convey to the members of the London Stock Exchange my cordial thanks for the expression of confidence contained in your telegram.—KITCHENER."

The Committee of the Manchester Stock Exchange yesterday passed a resolution that, " In view of the disgraceful and unpatriotic attacks on those responsible for the conduct of the war no copy of *The Times* or *Daily Mail* be allowed on the Manchester Stock Exchange." On the Newcastle-on-Tyne Exchange a resolution of confidence was passed in Lord Kitchener which stated that the members would rather be wrong with Lord Kitchener than right with the *Daily Mail.*

Right:
The story as covered by the Guardian.

Far right:
Northcliffe's own article. Monday, May 17th. The Times

ITALY

1922

An example of political censorship occurred when a book called *Viva Caporetto!* by Curzio Malaparte, published in 1921, laid the blame for the worst Italian defeat in 1917 during the First World War on '"the stupidity and incompetence of the officers". It was in effect a Socialist protest by the ordinary soldiers. When a second edition appeared in 1923 Fascists attacked bookshops in Rome – some said under the direct orders of Mussolini.'

When the Fascists came to power through their march on Rome in 1922 Mussolini personally assumed the post of Minister of the Interior and within a year had established censorship over the press and most publications, the object being to eliminate all critical comment on Fascism.

This photograph, taken in November 1922, shows that the Fascists did not need any legislation to destroy Socialist literature; they just got on with it, preceding Dr Goebbels by eleven years.

Ciano, Mussolini's son-in-law, was appointed in 1933 to be the Press Officer of the government and in 1938, inspired after a meeting

Italian fascists burning Socialist literature, 1922.

between Mussolini and Hitler, he launched a campaign against Italian Jews. He wrote in his diary, 'A first warning of the turning of the screw will be given by the bonfires of Jewish pro-Mason Francophile writings – Jewish writers and journalists will be banned from any activity – our resolution must now leave a mark on the customs of Italians. And they will have to learn to be less "sociable" in order to become harder, implacable, hateful. That is: masters.'

THE NAZIS

1933

30 January	Hindenburg, President of the Weimar Republic, appointed Adolf Hitler Chancellor.
4 February	The law for the Protection of the German People restricted the freedom of the press and dangerous material could be confiscated.
5 February	The HQ of the Communist Party was attacked and its library destroyed.
27 February	The burning of the Reichstag.
28 February	Hindenburg signed the Emergency Decree for the Defence of Nation and State which restricted freedom of speech, the freedom to meet in public, allowed letters and telephone calls to be intercepted and houses to be searched.
March	Dr Goebbels, who had taught briefly at Heidelberg University, read Greek classics, recited poems from memory, admired Friedrich Nietzsche and studied Marx's texts – particularly those directed against the bourgeoisie – became the head of the Reich Ministry for Enlightening the People and Propaganda.
7 April	The Law Relevant to State Government gave Goebbels control of schools and universities.
10 May	The burning of the books.

POLITICAL BURNING | **51** |

Throughout the early months of 1933 a campaign of vilification and intimidation was launched against Jews, Communists, Social Democrats, Trades Union leaders, Masons, sexual deviants and homosexuals. Its purpose was to purge all non-German elements in a crusade of national purification through which Germany would regain its pride and reinforce its culture, which had at its centre the German language embodying the soul of this great nation. It was a philosophical revival, a political revival, a nationalist revival and a military revival. The young were told it was their duty to purge their libraries of all decadent un-German books and the professors instructed them to attend the burnings. Fire was a means of purification – it had purified German politics through the burning of the Reichstag and now it would purify German culture.

The great burning took place on 10 May in the Opernplatz in Berlin and it was very carefully planned. A bonfire had been started in the evening and an hour before midnight books were passed from hand to hand along a human chain and thrown on to the flames. Vast amounts of books and manuscripts had been collected by students, including many Jewish books and those by certain authors who had been specifically selected – Heinrich Mann, Stefan Zweig, Freud, Erich Maria Remarque, Zola, Proust, Gide, Helen Keller and H.G. Wells. One archive that had been ransacked and was to provide 10,000 volumes was that of the Hirschfeld Institute of Sexual Science, which had been founded in 1919. It had a worldwide reputation, but the Nazis considered that it dealt only with degenerate perverts.

Bands had been laid on to accompany the students' songs, torches were provided for the marchers, news cameras had been summoned and the minister himself, Joseph Goebbels, was billed to make a speech at midnight, when he announced:

'The time has passed when the filth and impurities of Jewish sidewalk literature would fill the libraries. Therefore you have done well in the middle of this night to throw into the flames these unspiritual relics of the past. It is a strong, great and symbolic performance, a performance which should document for all the world: here the spiritual foundations of the November Weimar Republic sink to the ground. But out of these ruins there will arise the phoenix of the new spirit ... the past lies in the flames ... today under this sky and with these flames we take a new oath: the Reich and the Nation and our Leader, Adolf Hitler, Heil! Heil! Heil!'

Joseph Goebbels – The Fire Speech, 10 May 1933, film still.

Between 80,000 and 90,000 books were burnt that night and on the same day burnings were orchestrated across Germany, notably in the Romerberg in Frankfurt, the Königsplatz in Munich, the Schlossplatz in Breslau and in front of the Bismarck statue in Dresden. In 1935 Goebbels extended his censorship powers and by the time the war started 565 authors and 4,175 titles were banned.

One of the banned authors, Erich Kästner, actually attended the book burning as he felt he should 'bear witness'. Somebody recognised him and shouted out, 'Da ist Kästner' ('There is Kästner') and he pushed through the crowd and hurried away. Kästner's most famous book was *Emil and the Detectives* – that did not offend Goebbels, but what did was his 1931 novel *Fabian*, which described a bleak and corrupt post-war Germany and a Berlin which 'in the East resides crime, in the centre swindling, in the West lechery and to all points of the compass destruction lurks'. This occasioned the wrath of Goebbels: 'against decadence and decline in public morals. For breeding and good behaviour in the family and state! I consign to the flames the writing of Heinrich Mann, Ernst Gläser and Erich Kästner'. After the war, when Kästner learnt that the most common of the books confiscated from children as they arrived at Belsen and Dachau was *Emil and the Detectives* he burst into tears.

Magnus Hirschfeld had established in Berlin in 1919 his Institute for Sexual Science, an educational institution that became a communal centre for homosexuals, lesbians and a variety of sexual deviants. Hirschfeld himself had written a thousand-page book entitled *Die Homosexualität Des Mannes und Des Weibes* ('Homosexuality of Man and Woman'). He had also coined the phrase 'transvestism'. He rented out rooms in his office to supportive groups and occasionally to individuals, his most famous tenant being Christopher Isherwood. The Nazis had been keeping Hirschfeld under observation for several months and on Saturday 6 May Nazi students followed by members of the S.A. invaded the Institute and removed such a mass of books, photographs and medical records that trucks were needed. The books were to form a large part of the material thrown on to the bonfire four days later.

Hirschfeld was safe in Paris but he had been a double target for the Nazis as a Jew and as Berlin's most prominent homosexual. The rioters had also found a large bronze bust of him which they mounted on a stick and paraded to the bonfire, but it was not consumed as bronze melts between 1,900 and 2,100 degrees Fahrenheit, while paper burns at a much lower temerature. A street cleaner found the bust, took it home and kept it safe until the war was over, when he presented it to the Berlin Academy of Arts, where it is displayed today.

On that night of 10 May Christopher Isherwood was out in the crowds with his friend, the lecturer William Robson-Scott, where they saw the procession of students carrying the bronze bust and tossing it on the fire. When the books were thrown into the consuming flames, Isherwood cried, 'Shame', but 'not', he later admitted, 'very loudly'. Three days later he decided to leave Berlin for good.

Heinrich Mann's name was the third on a list issued the previous day, as he had been a Nazi target since February when advertising pillars in Berlin carried placards signed by him and Albert Einstein urging socialists and communists to unite against the Nazis. Mann's mistress, Nelly Kröger, a Communist sympathiser, urged him to get out as soon as possible. On 20 February she bought a ticket for him to go to Frankfurt and he left the next day, in just the clothes he stood up in. That was lucky, for on the following day the SS broke into his apartment. He went on to live in Los Angeles, where he died. In 1961 his remains were moved from the Santa Monica Woodlands Cemetery and cremated and his ashes were placed in an urn and taken back to East Berlin, where Walter Ulbricht, who was to become the builder of the Wall, declared, 'he belongs to us'.

One of the worst aspects of book burning in Fascist Germany and in Spain was that the enthusiastic ringleaders, usually students, were supported and encouraged by leading professors. The German Student Association helped to organise the May burning in Berlin and went on to organise thirty-four more burnings in university towns across Germany, leading the singing and giving the speeches.

On 6 April the German Student Union had posted a declaration for universities entitled 'The 12 Theses against the Un-German Spirit'. Thesis Four stated: 'The Jew can only think Jewish. If he writes German, he lies. The German who writes German, but thinks un-German, is a traitor. The student who speaks and writes un-German is furthermore thoughtless and unfaithful in duty.'

Pforzheim

Although Hitler did not receive the overall mandate he wanted in the Reichstag elections in March 1933 – he polled forty-four per cent of the vote – the Nazification of Germany started immediately after the results were announced. In his book *Wolfram: The Boy Who Went to War*, published in 2010, Giles Milton traced the history of the Aïchele family who lived in southern Germany near Pforzheim. They were middle-class, old-fashioned and nationalist – Wolfram's father was an artist and a freemason. They were not Jewish, but a Jewish magazine published his father's illustrations of wild animals. Within three days of the election Robert Wagner, a fanatical anti-Semite, was appointed the Reich commissar of the state of Baden. He assumed full police powers, arrested Socialist and Communist deputies, banned left-leaning papers and closed freemasons' lodges. Hermann Goering then banned the

Collecting books for burning on the Kaiser-Friedrich-Ufer in Hamburg, 15 May 1933.

magazine in which Wolfram's father's work appeared because it was published by a Jew.

In May Goebbels's dirt and shame books were burned in Pforzheim's market square. The favourite authors of Wolfram's mother, Heinrich Mann and Stefan Zweig, were thrown on to the flames and on several occasions the Gestapo forced their way into their house searching for more banned books, but his mother had hidden some of these under the dining-room floorboards. The local newspaper welcomed the burning: 'The difficult times went up with the flames. New life, new writing, new faith will blossom from the ashes.'

After the burning many Communists and Jews fled to Paris, where in 1934 a group, including Arthur Koestler, established in Montparnasse the Library of the Burnt Books. British supporters included H.G. Wells, Vera Brittain, Kingsley Martin, Naomi Mitchison and Bertrand Russell. The Library created a large archive of anti-Nazi material and became a centre for the study of Fascism. It did not survive the German occupation of Paris in 1940 and only one book from it is preserved in the Bibliothèque Nationale.

Further Fires

When the Nazis moved into Vienna in 1938 Jewish libraries and left-wing collections were seized. One institution that was to emerge with honour was Williams College in Massachusetts, which offered to buy the condemned books from the Vienna Library, but this offer was totally ignored. Some students in Vienna attempted to burn effigies of Hitler and the swastika but they were frustrated by Nazi sympathisers. Meanwhile in Germany the purging of libraries continued and many German writers were later to recall that in their schooldays there were burnings of books in the playgrounds – even though none of the books were actually in the school curriculum. Many other people simply purged their own libraries out of fear.

After the Nazi army had invaded Amsterdam, Louvain, Paris, Prague and Warsaw millions of books were destroyed. One Nazi gloated over the destruction of the famous library of the Lublin Yeshiva in 1939:

'For us it was a matter of special pride to destroy the Talmudic Academy, which was known as the greatest in Poland. We threw the large Talmudic library out of the building and carried the books to the marketplace where we set fire to them. The fire lasted twenty hours. The Lublin Jews assembled around and wept bitterly, almost silencing us with their cries. We summoned the military band and with joyful shouts the soldiers drowned out the sounds of the Jewish cries.'

THE HEARTFIELD MONTAGE

This is the photomontage by John Heartfield called *Durch Licht zur Nacht* ('Through Light to Night'). Thus spoke Dr Goebbels: 'Let us start new fires so that the dazzled do not awake.'

The oil can at the bottom right bears the name of Henri Deterding, the Dutch millionaire behind Shell who was a Nazi supporter, and the name of Goering, implying that he was responsible for the Reichstag fire. Apart from the works of Lenin and *Das Kapital* some of the books being burnt had been published by the left-wing publisher Wieland Herzfelde, with dust jackets designed by his brother Heartfield, like *Der Kaiser Gang, Die Generale Bleiben* ('The Kaiser Goes, the Generals Remain') (1932).

John Heartfield trained as a graphic artist in Munich before the First World War. He developed photomontage, which used photography as a political weapon to attack capitalism and the Nazis. Between 1930 and 1939 he published 237 photomontages in the magazine *AIZ* – the workers' illustrated paper. This had been published in Berlin but Heartfield fled to Prague in 1933 to escape the Nazis. He continued to publish *AIZ* in Prague, but in 1938 he had to flee again, this time to America.

The Cartoonists Got It Right

The general reaction of the world's press was of amazement rather than anger. Some took comfort that a heavy downpour of rain had damped down the affair and made it difficult to burn many of the books. It was dismissed as a childish, almost infantile action of 'witless students'; an act of stupidity rather than an exercise in evil. Few realised that they were witnessing the purpose, intensity and frenzy of the Nazi creed and some writers, like Bertolt Brecht, whose books had not been burnt, ironically asked for his to join the pyre. Others found some comfort in the famous passage from Milton's *Areopagitica* that books cannot be destroyed. Joseph Roth was one of the few to realise what was to come: 'We, who are German writers of Jewish blood, in these days when the smoke from our burning books is rising towards heaven, should recognise above all that we are defeated … we were in the front rows of those defending Europe and we were bludgeoned first.'

It was left to cartoonists across the world to express vividly the true horror of what had happened. Their images were more immediately powerful than column inches of comment. The Jewish community in New York were rather more alert to the dangers of what could follow, but the English press was rather muted and it was not until eight years later in 1941 that George Orwell made his famous comment that book burning was 'the most characteristic activity of the Nazis'.

'Once again the fires of hatred and of ignorance are kindled. Once again are flames seen rising from books given to destruction and the hurling of these volumes into blazing conflagrations is a throwback to dark ages after centuries of progress.'

The Throwback, 1933 by Nelson Harding (1879–1944).

"And they told me it was impossible to play a serious part with a mustache like mine."

Charlie Chaplin cartoon in the Daily Express, by Sidney Strube (1891–1956).

*'Hang and
Shoot'
cartoon from*
Leningradskaya
Pravda,
4 March 1933

*Neron …
en papier,
Paris.*

SPANISH FASCISM

Before the war in early 1934 anti-Catholic republicans, apart from destroying churches and killing priests, also burnt the libraries of convents and monasteries. In October 1934 an uprising in Asturias inspired by Franco sympathisers consigned to the flames books described as pornographic, revolutionary or immoral. 257 libraries of the poor were raided by the police and on 13 October the University of Asturias was burnt down. As Franco's troops extended their control over Spain so they extended their control over the printed word. Censorship was promulgated in 1936 and in 1937 the President of the State Technical Committee ordered libraries and cultural centres to purge their collections. In 1939 bookshops were allowed to reopen only after all their offending material had been destroyed.

Arriba España, Franco's nationalist propaganda paper, in its first number demanded, 'Comrade! You have the obligation to persecute Judaism, Masons, Marxism and separatism. Destroy and burn their newspapers, books, magazines and propaganda. Comrade! For the sake of God and the fatherland.' University City in Madrid was a target area; in Barcelona seventy-two tonnes of books were destroyed; in Navarre the local Fascist leader seized books from schools and libraries and burnt them.

'Arriba España' was first published in August 1936 and ended in June 1975, shortly before Franco's death.

But it was not one-sided: the Communists in charge of the Ministry of Public Education sent the archive of Madrid to be pulped – twenty-eight tonnes of records were destroyed.

The battle song of the Mateotti Battalion was:

Fascism is a vile enemy
Of peace and culture:
It suppresses books and schools
And is the graveyard of science.

One of the worst aspects of book-burning in Fascist Germany and Spain was that the enthusiastic ringleaders were usually students, who were supported and encouraged by leading academics. The very custodians of scholastic integrity and of the permanence of records and of academic freedom and of the right to study anything were the very ones who led the processions, sang the loudest, lit the bonfires and cheered hysterically.

Adolf Hitler and Francisco Franco heiling at the Meeting at Hendaye in the French Basque Country, 23 October, 1940.

MIKHAIL BULGAKOV (1891–1940)

'Manuscripts don't Burn'

In 1919 Mikhail Bulgakov abandoned his career as a doctor to devote his life to writing. Novels, plays and short stories flowed from his pen. He took a lively interest in current affairs, international problems and in the civil war that had broken out in the Ukraine, where he witnessed the fate of the intellectuals and the Tsarist army officers known as the White Guard. In May 1926 the secret police searched his flat in Moscow and seized his diary and the typescript of his novel *The Heart of a Dog*. He repeatedly asked for these to be returned and in 1930 he was successful, but on his death no diary was found and it was assumed that he must have burnt it. However, in the late 1980s a typed copy of his diary was discovered in the KGB archives and that led to it being published.

Bulgakov was interrogated on 22 September 1926 by OGPU – the predecessor of the KGB – just one day before the rehearsal of his play *The Days of the Turbins*, which covered the Ukrainian civil war and which was to transform his life. Stalin saw the play fifteen times, particularly liking the triumph of Bolshevism and at the end the singing of the Internationale. The play had been heavily censored – a scene where a Jew was tortured was cut out, but the intelligentsia of the Ukraine were portrayed sympathetically, and although the White Guards lost they could even be seen as the heroes of this Ukrainian tragedy. In 1929 Stalin condemned Bulgakov's work as anti-Soviet and all his plays were banned. So in 1930, in a letter to the government, Bulgakov protested about this censorship, saying that in an act of despair he had thrown 'the draft of a novel about the devil into a stove'. He also asked permission to leave the Soviet Union, which was refused.

In 1930, out of the blue, he received a telephone call from Stalin himself, who clearly did not want such a talented writer to leave the Soviet Union. In this telephone call Bulgakov admitted that he could not write about Russia other than by living there and so, to help him, Stalin arranged for him to have a new post in the Moscow Art Theatre. They never spoke again.

Stalin's interest in Bulgakov's work probably saved his life but it did not give him the freedom that he wanted, for the threat of persecution, internal exile or prison was ever present. The censorship continued and he referred to his 'killed plays' – after a few years even *The Days of the Turbins* was no longer performed. In a letter to a friend in April 1932 he advised him to be cautious and burn the notes that he had received, adding 'pechka davno uzhe sdelalas' moei lyubimoi redakstsie' ('the stove has long been my favourite editor').

Bulgakov's masterpiece, which he worked on and re-edited for over twelve years, *The Master and Margarita*, was withheld from publication following Stalin's declaration that Bulgakov's work was anti-Soviet. Even after Bulgakov's death in 1940 it was not published in full until 1973, though certain passages had been published in 1966. It was to become Russia's bestseller. It is a superb tour de force, mixing fantasy and science fiction with an amazing interplay of magic and reality, which amounts to a satirical attack upon the arid dictatorship of Soviet Russia. In it, the Master has written a book about Pilate and a Christ-like figure which the Soviet Union of Writers, the guardians of social realism, the new cultural orthodoxy, refuses to allow to be published, and the State censors are depicted as comical, ignorant oafs. Desperate and frightened and even seeking sanctuary for a time in the lunatic asylum, the Master tears up the pages violently, throwing them into a stove. After a satanic ball, Wolland, a satanic, godlike figure, restores the text by magic with a superb declaration of defiance: 'Manuscripts don't burn'. This became the most famous quotation, affirming that the pen is mightier than the sword and that a work of art can outlive

Mikhail Bulgakov in 1928 during the period when he worked in secret on his undisputed masterpiece, The Master and Margarita.

Photo courtesy of Lebrecht Music & Arts

a political regime. It has been estimated that in 1991, the year of the collapse of the Soviet Union, one book in ten published in Russia was by Bulgakov.

Bulgakov's Message Lives Today

In 2013 a film entitled *Manuscripts Don't Burn* was made by the Iranian writer and director Mohammed Rasoulof. It won the International Critics' Prize at the Cannes Film Festival in May. This was based upon events during one of the notorious crackdowns by the Ayatollahs called the Chain Murders, 1988–89, when artists were arrested, disappeared or were murdered. It reveals a chilling drama of a series of killings where one victim, paralysed by fear through interrogations, betrays another and so on. Rasoulof was sentenced 'for acting against national security', whereupon he replied from the dock, 'You are acting against national security by condemning artists.' After a month in solitary confinement he managed to escape with his family to Hamburg. The Ayatollahs did not need to burn books when they could kill the authors.

YIANNIS RITSOS (1909–1990)

1936

The Greek poet Yiannis Ritsos was a left-wing activist who in 1931 joined the Communist Party. In 1936 he published his most famous poem, *Epitaphios*, a funeral lament. A strike by tobacco workers in Thessalonica had been violently suppressed by the police who fired upon the crowd killing thirty people and wounding another 300. The most striking photograph of the event showed a grieving mother in black weeping over the dead body of her son in the street – it was a Pietà.

It inspired the twenty-seven-year-old poet to write a long lyrical poem based upon the chant that was sung in the Greek Orthodox Church on the evening of Good Friday. *Epitaphios* is the name for the cloth that dresses the funeral bier of Christ in the Good Friday processions in Greek Orthodox Churches. In this poem Mary and her

*A grieving
mother weeps
over the slain
body of Tasos
Tousis, on
the corner of
Egnatia Street
and Venizelou
Street in
Thessalonica in
1936.*

*Yiannish Ritsos
at Eri Ritsou
Mpenaki
Museum.*

crucified son grieve and lament over the body of the mother's son, and in writing it Ritsos turned the local struggle into a universal struggle for social justice. The poem also challenged the values of a country which called itself Christian but killed those who fought for justice. The son lives on in the lives of his comrades and the mother vows to take up his struggle. In a translation of a couplet by Amy Mims:

> Now you are shrouded in banners. My child, now go to sleep.
> I'm on my way to your brothers, bearing your voice with me.

The general industrial unrest led to the dictatorship of Ionnis Metaxas, who seized power in 1936. He outlawed *Epitaphios* and rounded up the remaining 250 copies in Athens, which were burnt in public at the foot of the Acropolis.

In 1958 the exiled Greek composer Mikis Theodorakis, known in the West for his music for *Zorba the Greek*, set *Epitaphios* to music and it became the anthem of the Greek Left. When in 1963 the young left-wing Deputy Grigorios Lambrakis was dying in hospital after a murderous assault, a big crowd led by Ritsos and Theodorakis gathered in the street and sang the *Epitaphios*. In 1969 this event was turned into a cult movie, Z, by the renowned Greek film director Costa Gavras.

In 1967, when the Colonels seized power in Greece, this time they did not burn *Epitaphios*, they exiled Ritsos to Samos.

ANIMAL FARM

1947

In 1947 T.S. Eliot, then editor at Faber, George Orwell's publisher, turned down *Animal Farm* as it was too 'Trotskyite'. Orwell fared no better with Victor Gollancz, publisher of the Left Book Club, Jonathan Cape or the Dial Press in New York, which told him that stories about animals had no market in America. So much for Walt Disney! Eventually a small English publisher, Secker & Warburg, took the risk of publication, paying Orwell just £45 for what was to become a

Animal Farm, *Munich jacket for the Ukranian*
edition (from a Blackwell's catalogue).

worldwide classic. Such is its political power that *Animal Farm* has even now not been published in China, Burma, North Korea, Iran or most of the Muslim world. In Zimbabwe an edition that made Napoleon, the pig dictator, wear President Robert Mugabe's black horn-rimmed glasses led to the offices of the publishers being blown up.

Some Ukrainian and Polish Socialists who were living in refugee camps approached Orwell to see whether he would give them permission to produce a copy in Ukrainian. Orwell willingly agreed and did not charge them for it, as he recognised that although they were Socialists they were opposed to Stalin's dictatorship. In 1947 2,000 copies were printed in Munich under the title *Kolgosp Tvarin* and distributed to the refugees. More editions quickly followed in other East European languages, but the American military authorities in Germany and Austria considered that it was propaganda printed on an illegal press. They collected 1,500 copies and handed them to the Red Army to be burnt – ironically reflecting the end of the novel, where the pigs and the farmers join forces.

HAROLD MACMILLAN (1894–1986)

1957

Coming from a family that had founded one of the leading publishers in England, Harold Macmillan not only enjoyed reading – Trollope was his favourite – but he revelled in writing. His letters to his mother when he was a soldier in the trenches in World War I were, in effect, his war diaries and in 1981 he published the diary that he had kept when he was Minister Resident in Algiers, Greece and Italy from 1943 to 1945.

From 1950 to 1956 Macmillan kept a diary. He started at a time when he sensed that Labour's term of in office was coming to an end and in the new Tory government he would have a seat in the Cabinet. These diaries run to twenty-two volumes of black-bound, foolscap notebooks, but they stop abruptly on 4 October 1956. In the summer of that year Nasser had nationalised the Suez Canal, and the diaries record Macmillan's view that 'Nasser should not be allowed to get away with it' and the role that he had as Chancellor of the Exchequer in formulating a policy that would lead to an invasion of Egypt. He was quite clearly a hawk, meeting Foster Dulles, the American Secretary of State, and President Eisenhower on several occasions to overcome their reluctance to invade and to secure America's financial support for the UK in the event of an invasion.

However, there is a gap covering October, November, December and January and he resumed the diary only on 3 February 1957, by which time he had become Prime Minister, succeeding Anthony Eden. So there is no record of the plan that Israel had worked out with France for an invasion of Egypt, nor the collusion with Israel in this plan, nor the reaction of America and the world to the invasion of Suez. This took place on 29 October 1956 and was called off on 6 November, followed by the collapse of Anthony Eden's health and his resignation. Macmillan's diary is silent about his role in all of this. During this time he moved from being a hawk to a dove and, as some have said, 'Macmillan was the first in and the first out'. We will never quite know.

Maurice Harold MacMillan, 1st Earl of Stockton (1894–1986).

Macmillan started his diary again on 3 February 1957, writing that events 'began to move with such a speed and with such pressure upon us all that I was not able to keep up the diary'. But later he told his biographer, Alistair Horne, that he had destroyed the diary at the specific request of Anthony Eden and I suspect that being rather old-fashioned he would almost certainly have burnt it himself.

It is extraordinary that MacMillan, after a very long day as Prime Minister, would settle down and write in longhand a detailed record of the issues he had dealt with. It is surprising how much of his time was spent on foreign affairs – Cuba, Europe, De Gaulle – and on the Empire and Commonwealth – Nigeria, Aden, Sierra Leone, India, Tanganyika, Uganda and the West Indies. There were sparse comments on domestic politics and his reluctance to comment very much on personalities made the diaries rather flat – they are very dissimilar from the more vivid diaries of Barbara Castle and Richard Crossman.

The later diaries from 1957 come to life in 1963, when Macmillan had decided to stand down as Prime Minister before the 1964 election, and they reveal the very great interest he took in whoever was going to succeed him. Initially he favoured Hailsham, as Maudling, the Chancellor, was too uninspiring and R.A. Butler was too weak. But when Macmillan during the Tory Party Conference had to go into hospital in October 1963 for a prostate operation, his records become infinitely more detailed and reveal how he manoeuvred to secure the succession of Alec Douglas-Home. That he was prepared to record for posterity.

Macmillan also engaged in some personal burning relating to correspondence between his wife Dorothy and Robert Boothby MP, with whom she had had a long affair which Macmillan knew about. Long after Dorothy died in 1966 Boothby in his flat in Eaton Square burnt over 700 letters from her. Macmillan found a lot of Boothby's letters at Birch Grove and told him that he had not read them but that he would burn them as 'I didn't want some Arizonian professor writing a thesis about you and me'. The fireplace at Birch Grove was apparently too small and Macmillan had to use the garden incinerator, but the wind got up and he had to chase after pieces of the letters that were swirling away.

In 1959, just two years later, Macmillan had to resume full diplomatic relations with Egypt and paid them compensation.

Cartoon by Vicky (1913–1966), 4 May 1957.

CLEANING THE COLONIAL RECORD

1958–1962

Towards the end of 2013 the government released documents which showed that the Colonial Office in the late 1950s and early 1960s instituted a policy to destroy certain records relating to those countries that were to become independent, such as Kenya and Malaya. The purpose was to avoid any embarrassment to the British government over such matters as the way in which the Mau Mau rebellion in Kenya and the guerrilla campaign in Malaya had been suppressed.

Kenya became independent in 1962 and officials were asked to form three-man teams of 'European descent' to identify and destroy groups of documents that might embarrass the government, embarrass the police or army, or endanger the security agencies, since these papers might fall into the hands of the newly independent country and be used against Britain. Clearly there was much to hide, for fifty-one years later in 2013, the UK government paid £20 million to Kenyans whose torture or abuse had been documented.

In Malaya the destruction of records seems to have been on a massive scale. The search was so wide that officials recognised that the purpose was to withdraw embarrassing papers but 'we cannot advise you what is and what is not likely to be embarrassing'. The papers were burnt in the Royal Naval incinerator at Singapore, which received on one occasion five lorry-loads of files.

Sir Donald MacGillivray was one of the most distinguished figures in the Colonial Service and had served in a number of trouble spots: Palestine, Jamaica and as High Commissioner in Malaya from 1952 to 1957, taking over just after his predecessor had been assassinated. He would have had an intimate knowledge of the Malaya insurgency, which had started in December 1948 when a Scots Guards platoon executed twenty-four perfectly harmless Chinese plantation workers. This was an insane act which fortunately was never repeated. The insurgency was a war of skirmishes and attrition that had not been completely cleared up at the time of Malaya's independence in 1957. MacGillivray would also have been aware of what is considered one of the most successful engagements in Britain's colonial history, by

Sir Donald MacGillivray. Still in charge...

Sir Gerald Templer from 1952 to 1954 when he wiped out more than two thirds of the Communist guerrillas. It was a very intense operation, involving over 40,000 British troops and Special Branch operatives. In a letter to Tunku Abdul Rahman, Sir Donald wrote, 'the removal of these documents is in accord with the usual policy by which the secret records of one government are not left for the use of its successors'.

MAO'S CULTURAL REVOLUTION

1966–1976

From the moment he took power in 1949 'with a dictatorship of the proletariat' China's Communist leader Mao Zedong waged war against China's historic past, scholars, writers and intellectuals. In 1951 he launched the Thought Reform Campaign with this declaration:

But will not Marxism destroy any creative impulses? It will; it will certainly destroy the creative impulses that arise from feudal, bourgeois and petty-bourgeois ideology, from liberalism, individualism and nihilism, from art-for-art's sake, from the aristocratic, decadent and pessimistic outlook – indeed any creative impulse that is not rooted in the people and the proletariat. So far as proletarian artists and writers are concerned, should not these impulses be utterly destroyed? I think these should; indeed they must be utterly destroyed and while they are being destroyed, new things can be built up.

This was intensified when in 1966 Mao launched the Great Proletarian Cultural Revolution. All non-Communist ideas, all writings that did not conform to Marxist-Leninist principles were to be destroyed together with the people who had dared to express them. As for intellectuals, they were the 'stinking element' who were to be eliminated by students called the Red Guards, each waving Mao's *Little Red Book*, for to them Mao was a god.

Across China hundreds of thousands of books were destroyed in bonfires and a former Red Guard, Yan, in 1996 described just one of these:

Finally the books – by now a small mountain – were set on fire by the Red Guards.... Excited and passionate slogans accompanied the thick smoke rising up into the sky. Perhaps the Red Guards felt that the act of merely burning books was not 'revolutionary' enough. In any case, using their belts, they prodded the 'Black Gang' [instructors] to the edge of the fire and made them stand there with their heads lowered, bodies bent forward, to be fried in the raging flames of the Great Cultural Revolution.... What I witnessed was the Beijing N0.11 Middle School Red Guard book fire.'

Another Red Guard student described what had happened at the Nan Yang Model Middle School in Shanghai:

'Now this centre of education had become the new frontier of the war that had been declared on civilization. On the playground, the road, the roof of the library, even under the grapevines in the school's vineyards, people were burning books. The sky turned red.'

Teachers and scholars were tortured or given menial jobs like latrine cleaners. So great was the fervour of the guards that in many cases not only were books destroyed, but libraries and buildings were torn down. Private houses were invaded and books burnt in their gardens. In 1986 the former Red Guard Cheng recalled:

'I looked out the window and saw bright, leaping flames in the garden. A bonfire had been lit in the middle of the garden and the Red Guards were standing around the fire carelessly tossing my books on to the flames. My heart tightened with pain.'

The burning of the Four Olds – Old Ideas, Old Customs, Old Books, Old Habits, 1966–1976.

The Cultural Revolution was a recognition that Communism had failed and had led to a ravaged and devastated society. Yet Mao, 'the Great Helmsman', was not blamed. After his death, the scapegoats were the Gang of Four, who had a show trial in 1980. China continues to control the version of modern history that it wants its people to read.

THE HUTTON REPORT

2004

On Saturday 21 January 2004 a copy of Lord Hutton's report was burnt in Whitehall close to the entrance of Downing Street by a group of anti-war protesters led by George Galloway, who had been expelled from the Labour Party for his opposition to the Iraq War.

    After the fall of Saddam Hussein, Lord Justice Hutton was appointed by the Blair Government on 18 July 2004, the day after the dead body of David Kelly was found in a wood, to investigate 'the circumstances surrounding the death of David Kelly'.

Observer,
1 February 2004,
front page photograph by Alessandro Abbonizio.

On 29 May 2004 Andrew Gilligan, a BBC journalist, alleged that the government's dossier published in February justifying the case of the war had been embellished with misleading exaggerations of Iraq's military capability, and specifically that Hussein had 'weapons of mass destruction' that could be launched within forty-five minutes and would reach London. This became known as the 'Dodgy Dossier', and the allegation was repeated on two other BBC programmes. In the furore that followed the source of this information was traced to David Kelly, an experienced United Nations weapons inspector in Iraq, and Blair agreed that his name should be publicly revealed. The intense media and political interest was too much for David Kelly and he committed suicide.

The Hutton Report cleared the government of any wrongdoing and strongly criticised the BBC, which led to the resignation of the Chairman and the Director-General, Greg Dyke – though later he bitterly regretted resigning. The tables had been turned and the BBC was in the dock. Most newspapers immediately called the report a whitewash and the *Independent* published a completely blank front page. Hutton did not examine or challenge the intelligence and the intelligence services escaped censure, but Hutton did say that Alastair Campbell, Tony Blair's Director of Communications and Strategy, had no hand in 'sexing-up' the dossier.

RELIGIOUS
BURNING

THE CRUSADE AGAINST THE CATHARS

1209–45

'They burned them with joy in their hearts'

PETER OF LES VAUX DE CERNAY

What came to be called the Albigensian Heresy was established at several places in Languedoc, notably at Albi, Carcassonne, Béziers and Narbonne, where the people who believed in it were known as Cathars. They believed in dualism – there was not one god but two – a good god and a bad god, because a good god would never have inflicted suffering on the people he created, for that was the work of the bad god. As a result Cathars did not believe in redemption and therefore there was no need for Christ, who had been created by the bad god. This total denial of Christianity was in the eyes of the Catholic Church 'a damnable heresy'.

Innocent III was elected Pope in 1198 and became one of the most powerful and determined of the medieval popes, interfering with the internal politics of the German states and France. In England he forced the King, known as John Lackland, to acknowledge him as his overlord, and invited the King of France, Philip Augustus, to seize the kingdom of England. He showed the same vigour in protecting the authority of the papacy on all religious matters, and for him stamping out heresies was a sacred duty.

In 1209 Pope Innocent III launched a crusade against the Cathars. The Crusaders this time were French feudal lords, led by Simon de Montfort, who, having been stripped of his estates by King John, looked upon Languedoc as an area they could pillage and whose lands they could seize. Their campaigns against the Duke of Toulouse, the lesser princelings and lords of the cities were excessively savage. The first city to fall was Béziers where the whole of the population was massacred by the crusaders, inspired by the words of the Papal legate, the Abbot of Cîteaux, 'Kill them all, God will know his own'. Carcassonne's entire population was expelled. It was after the fall of Minerve Castle in July 1210 that Simon de Montfort imposed the punishment of death by burning on 140 Cathars, and in 1215 the Pope recognised his right to Toulouse. This series of massacres amounted to a holocaust.

One of the great concerns of Innocent III was that the Cathars used their own language, Occitan, which was the language of the peasants and which therefore common people could understand when much of the worship and rituals of the Catholic Church were conducted in Latin. It therefore became crucial to stamp out this language. It was not just the heretics who were burnt, but the whole written record of Catharism was systematically destroyed and only three fragments have survived: two written in Occitan and one in Latin. So the knowledge that we have of Catharism is gleaned from the meticulous records kept by the interrogation of the heretics by the inquisitors.

The crusade soon developed into a series of local fights in which Toulouse and many other towns changed hands several times. These battles went on until 1245 and were conducted with exceptional

The expulsion of the Cathars from Carcassonne, 15 August 1209.

savagery, followed by severe reprisals when many were tortured to death or burnt at the stake. Indeed, the last mass burning of Cathars took place in Carcassonne a hundred years later, in 1329. The Inquisition was established in Toulouse in 1233 and its excesses were so gruesome – even the dead were exhumed to be burnt – that revolts took place in many of the towns: but the Inquisition never gave up.

THE MIRACLE OF FANJEAUX

1207

In the twelfth century the Albigensian heresy and its adherents, the Cathars, had become deeply embedded in south-west France. There were many powerful interests in this region – the attempts by a number of French kings to exert their sovereignty over it, the ambitions and rivalries of many local nobles and even the marauding interests of Spanish adventurers led by Ferdinand of Aragon, all played a part. Above all there was the determination of the Pope to stamp out what was seen as a loathsome, evil religion.

The Miracle of Fanjeaux was the last attempt to resolve the dispute between the Catholic Church and the Cathars before the call to arms. In 1206 a Spanish preacher, Dominigo de Guzmán, saw a fireball fall from the sky and, proclaiming it a miracle, he founded a monastery near the town of Montreal. In the following year a conference was summoned in that town which was meant to lead to a peaceful debate between the Cathars, led by Esclarmonde de Foix, the High Priestess of the Cathars, the daughter of the Count of Foix, pitched against Dominigo, for the Catholic Church. The conference did not get off to a good start when the Catholic prelate told Esclarmonde 'to return to her spinning'. Dominigo, who was later to establish an order of preachers and be sanctified as St Dominic, placed a page from the Bible and a Cathar parchment side by side on the hot coals in a public 'ordeal by fire'. The parchment burnt to ashes while the pages from the Bible flew up to the rafters, scorching the roof, clearly proof positive that Catholicism was recognised by God and that the cult of the Cathars should recognise this divine sign or there would be the most dire results.

The Burning of Books or St Dominic and the Albigensians, by Pedro Berruguete, c.1495.

THE SPANISH INQUISITION

1478–1834

'I myself hardly ever read a book without feeling a mood to give it a good censoring.'
ROBERT BELLARMINE, CARDINAL INQUISITOR, 1598

Ferdinand and Isabella appointed the first Inquisitors on 27 September 1480 and thereby created an ecclesiastical court that answered to the kings of Spain, not to the Pope; it was to last until 1834. Its initial role was to force the Jews who had become Christians, known as Conversos, to be fully absorbed into Spanish society by showing that they had abandoned all aspects of Judaism – customs, dress and food. In 1492 Torquemada, the ascetic, Dominican fanatic, full of pitiless zeal, who had become the Grand Inquisitor, persuaded the monarch to expel all Jews from Spain because they had prevented the Conversos from being fully assimilated.

From the beginning all books in Hebrew, including of course many copies of the Talmud and the Torah, were seized or burnt. This was quickly followed by the burning of Jews – 700 between the years 1481–88. In 1499 another ascetic priest, Cisneros, the confessor to Queen Isabella and later Regent of Spain, turned his attention to the Moors still living in Granada, which had been occupied by the Spanish in 1492. When Cisneros discovered that there were not many converts from Islam to Christianity – those that had were known as Moriscos – he personally launched a campaign of forcible baptism. On 12 October 1501 the Sovereign ordered the destruction of all Qur'ans in Granada – in total 5,000 were burnt. In 1511 the Inquisition went further by prohibiting the reading and publication of any books in Arabic.

The third heretic group to be persecuted by the Inquisition was the Lutherans, and again that started with books. When a few Lutheran books began to circulate in the 1520s the Inquisition pounced and printing works and bookshops were regularly inspected. In 1524 a Flemish vessel docking in San Sebastian was found to have two barrels of Lutheran books, which were burnt on the beach. In 1525 the crew of a Venetian ship were arrested for attempting to land a cargo of Protestant texts and in 1531 even a pedlar was tried for distributing such books. In January 1558 there was another major burning of books seized from heretics at Valladolid and the last of these events occurred at Toledo on 29 June 1634. The Catholic Church had decided it wasn't enough to expel both the Jews and the Moors: the very faith they practised had to be obliterated from the face of the earth, or at least the Spanish earth. It took a long time for Rome to realise the futility of such persecution.

The working practices of the Inquisition were as ruthless as those of Stalin and Hitler. The accused were isolated in prison; not allowed to see their informers; given no knowledge of the specific charges against them; tortured and forced to confess; their families threatened; their property seized; and most were put to death. The only difference that the executions were not in private but at large public ceremonies – the Auto da Fe – the first of which was held in Seville on 6 February 1481, when six Conversos were burnt at the stake. These great public spectacles were to show the whole community what fate would befall those who stepped out of line.

The Inquisition became one of the central agencies of the Catholic Church, establishing a vast bureaucracy in European countries and extending its reach into Mexico and Goa. The most ardent and active pursuers of heretics were the white-robed Dominican friars and they lived up to their Latin tag, *Domini Canes* – 'The Hounds of God'. Torquemada, who was a Dominican friar, wrote its first rule book, setting out the procedures for exposing heretics and their examination. That was followed by another Dominican, Nicholas Eymerich, who wrote the *Directorium Inquisitorium* – a manual that detailed all the techniques of torture and at what stage they should be applied. This was necessary and justified, for Pope Innocent IV in 1252 had issued the Papal Bull *Ad Extirpanda* which first authorised the use of torture against heretics.

JEWISH BOOKS

1507–21

A campaign was started at Cologne University in 1507 by Johannes Pfefferkorn, a Jew who had converted to Christianity, to destroy all Jewish books. The Emperor Maximilian I ordered the Jews to give to Pfefferkorn all books opposing Christianity and all Jewish books, apart from the Old Testament.

An early target was the library of the synagogue in Frankfurt, which was saved only when the Jews appealed to the Archbishop of Mainz (who owed them a considerable sum of money) and he intervened, but the seizures went on until 1510. This campaign was opposed by a distinguished Humanist scholar, Johannes Reuchlin, who specialised in Hebrew and Greek studies, arguing that Jewish

Woodcut,
Cologne, 1521.

books were not blasphemous or heretical and an understanding of them was useful in the mission to convert Jews. He also reminded the Emperor how vital an understanding of Hebrew was to the study of the scriptures.

Reuchlin was viciously attacked and had to defend himself before the Inquisition. His position became worse when the University of Cologne in 1520 condemned him, prior to its campaign to drive Jews out of Germany – just as they had been driven out of England in 1290, France in 1394, Spain in 1492 and Portugal in 1497. The dispute was referred to Rome and for a time in 1516 it looked as if Leo X, particularly as Rome had become the centre for Christian scholarship on Judaism, would favour Reuchlin. But the Dominicans managed to delay the finding and by 1520 the judgement went against him. Pfefferkorn immediately called for Reuchlin to be burnt along with his works and other Jewish books.

Reuchlin was to die a year later, but by then the papacy had decided that with the challenge of Martin Luther they had bigger fish to fry and more important books to burn.

MEXICO, THE AZTEC CIVILISATION

1519

When the Spanish privateer Hernando Cortés, with a small number of soldiers – conquistadors – discovered Mexico, they found the flourishing Aztec civilisation, which had large public buildings including many temples, huge wealth, books and a set of beliefs with rituals and idols which the Spanish considered to be little more than magic. After the initial pillaging and plunder they decided to destroy ruthlessly and systematically this civilisation once and for all.

In 1527 Charles V, the Holy Roman Emperor and King of Spain, appointed Zumarraga as the first Bishop of Mexico and in 1530 at Texcoco, the Athens of the Aztecs, there was a great bonfire of Aztec books, idols and pictures. The books were created on paper derived from the bark of a fig tree and the Aztec language was depicted in glyphs and pictograms, recording their history and culture in a series of codices which the Spaniards looked upon as magic symbols promoting pagan superstition, and so they were burnt. They took care, however, to send to Rome some of the codices so that the nature of the heresy could be identified, recorded and studied. As a result many of the foundation documents of the Aztec civilisation can now be found in various European cities.

Franciscan friars burning Aztec books and clothing, 1582.

Incendio de todas las ropas y libros y atavios de los sacerdotes ydolatras y se los quemaron los frayles

A fellow Franciscan monk, Diego de Landa, who had been a student of Cardinal Cisneros, the Chief Inquisitor in Spain, fervently followed Zumarraga with a huge bonfire at Mani in the Yucatán in 1562, when twenty seven codices and idols were burnt. The Aztec language was suppressed in favour of Castilian, the first grammar of which had been published in 1492 with the comment that 'language is always the partner of Empire'.

This illustration comes from a codex – *Historia de Tlaxcala*. It was written between 1581 and 1584 by the Tlaxcaltecan historian Diego Munoz Camargo, in two languages – Spanish and native Nahuatl – and it was probably intended as a gift for Philip II. It was written on European paper using pen and china ink and bound in vellum. It also comprised 157 images of the history of the people.

As the province of Tlaxcala had not been conquered by the Aztecs, the Spanish looked upon it as an ally and Camargo's *Historia* relates the battles that the Spanish waged against the Aztecs and how they were determined to impose Christianity upon a pagan, godless people. This extraordinary book was bought in Spain in the eighteenth century by Dr William Hunter, who bequeathed it to Glasgow University.

Diego de Landa, archbishop of Yucatán
The curse of God upon his pious soul –
Placed all their Devil's picture books under ban
And, piling them in one sin-heap, burned the whole;

But he took the trouble to keep the calendar
By which the Devil had taught them to count time.
The impious creatures tallied back as far
As ninety million years before Eve's crime.

That was enough: they burned the Mayan books,
Saved souls and kept their own in proper trim.
Diego de Landa in heaven always looks
Towards God: God never looks at him.

A.D. HOPE, AUSTRALIAN POET

PAPAL BULL, 1520

Martin Luther

Before the invention of printing by Gutenberg in Mainz in 1440 the burning of a book was an effective way for the Church to suppress heresy, as so few copies of it existed. The art of writing was confined to a handful of scholars – all of whom had been trained by the Church and most of whom worked in monastic libraries – and so the capacity to produce duplicates was very limited. This was why the heresy of Jan Hus in Bohemia, which challenged papal power, was so ruthlessly crushed – he simply couldn't get enough support.

Although China had invented printing, Gutenberg's press of moveable metal type allowed a printed work to be set up and printed much more quickly. By 1500 there were 200 printing shops in Germany and the man who realised their potential to spread his views was Martin Luther.

Luther's anger at the selling by the Dominican monk Tetzel of papal indulgences for the remission of sins had built up over years, but became a public outrage when on All Saints' Day, 31 October 1517, he nailed his *95 Theses* on the church door of the Castle Church of Wittenberg and, suitably for a scholastic debate, wrote them in Latin.

What had started as an attack upon the power, wealth and corruption of the papacy became a movement that made the Bible the sole source of religious authority and also available to ordinary people in their own language. The papacy realised the potential danger of this and Pope Leo X, who had dismissed Luther as 'a drunken German who will change his mind when sober' excommunicated him. On 10 December 1520 just before the Papal Bull *Ex Serge Domine* arrived in Wittenberg some students had started to burn books by scholastic authors near the east gate of the university. Luther joined the students at the bonfire and threw the Papal Bull and the Church of Rome's ecclesiastical laws on to the flames. Less than a month later he was excommunicated by the Pope.

By throwing the Bull on to a fire Luther used the very weapon of the Church – for his own works had been burnt by the Papal Nuncio Alexander. It was a dramatic, defiant and impertinent act – but it was to change the course of history. At the Confrontation of Worms in 1521, ordered by the Holy Roman Emperor Charles V, Luther uttered his famous declaration, 'Hier stehe ich. Ich can nicht anders. Gott helfe mir.' ('Here I stand – I can do nothing else – God help me').

Between 1517 and 1521 when the famous Edict of Worms ordered the burning of his books, Luther had printed thirty sermons and other works in some 370 editions. These were burnt in St Paul's Churchyard in London in 1521, where the fire was watched by Cardinal Wolsey and the Papal ambassadors. Luther had already been working with a Wittenberg printer, Johann Grunenberg, which meant that each edition could be as large as a thousand copies – showing the speed and flexibility of the Gutenberg press – and it led to over 300,000 copies in German, not Latin, being circulated in Europe. From 1521–1545 Luther's output was prolific; indeed he was the author of half of the pro-Reformation publications. It was

Luther burning the Papal Bull and the books of Church laws, 10 December 1520.

*Tit for Tat –
Pope Leo X
supervising
the burning of
Martin Luther's
books after the
first Diet of
Worms, 1521.*

the printing press that allowed the Reformation to spread and made the burning of books as a means of destroying heresy unnecessary, ineffective and meaningless.

However, burning retained a certain symbolic status. When the Qur'an was published in Latin in Basle the city council banned it and seized all available copies to burn them. But it was Luther who

protested, arguing that Christians should read the Qur'an to see 'how entirely cursed, abominable and desperate a book it is, full of lies, fables and abominations that the Turks conceal and gloss over' and urged the city authorities 'to vex the devil, set the book free and don't withhold it ... one must open sores and wounds in order to heal them'. Compared to Salman Rushdie's *Satanic Verses*, published some 400 years later, this was a pinprick, for there was no ayatollah around to order Luther's assassination.

The translation of the Bible into English by William Tyndale in 1526 was followed by several other versions. One that James I of England wanted to stop was the Calvinists' Geneva Bible, which had first appeared in 1506. However he did not order it to be burnt, but instead he commissioned a team of forty-seven scholars to produce 'an authorised version' and when that was published in 1611 it became known as the King James Bible: one of the greatest works in English literature.

TYNDALE'S BIBLE

1536

William Tyndale was a theologian, a Catholic priest and a leading scholar, fluent in several languages including Greek, Latin, Hebrew and German. At the age of twelve he went to Magdalen School in Oxford and then to the College, studying there for eight years. In 1522, when he acquired a copy of Martin Luther's New Testament in German, he was inspired to begin his English translation. Tyndale sought the approval of the Bishop of London, Cuthbert Tunstall, for an English version of the Bible, but he was told that would be heretical. So in 1524 he moved to northern Europe, living a rather nomadic life trying to keep ahead of the forces of the Catholic Church and the Holy Roman Emperor. He was never to set foot in England again. With an astonishing commitment and passion he set about translating the New Testament and arranged for it to be printed in Worms in 1526; he revised it and published two further editions in 1534 and 1536.

cxix.

The Gospell off Sancte Jhon.

The fyrst Chapter.

In the begynnynge was that worde/ ād that worde was with god: and god was thatt worde. The same was in the begynnynge wyth god. All thyngꝭ were made by it/ and with out it/ was made noo thige/ that made was. In it was lyfe/ And lyfe was the light of mē/ And the light shyneth i darcknes/ ād darcknes cōpreheded it not.

There was a mā sent from god/ whose name was Jhon. The same cā as a witnes/ to beare witnes of the light/ that all men through hi myght beleve. He was nott that light: but to beare witnes of the light. That was a true light/ which lighteneth all men that come ito the worlde. He was in the worlde/ ād the worlde by hi was made: and the worlde knewe hym not.

He cā ito his awne/ ād his received hi not. vns to as meny as received hi/ gave he power to be the sones of god: i that they beleved ō his name: which were borne not of bloude nor of the will of the flesshe/ nor yet of the will of men: but of god. And that worde was made flesshe/ and dwelt amonge vs/ and we sawe the glory off yt/ as the glory off the only begotten sonne off the father/

Copies began to circulate in England in the late 1520s, drawing down upon Tyndale the wrath of Henry VIII, 'The Defender of the Faith', Cardinal Wolsey and Thomas More – the great heretic hunter who attacked Tyndale viciously, descending at times to coarse scatology. In the early 1530s, when Henry VIII had decided to break from Rome and had married the Protestant Anne Boleyn, he asked Thomas Cromwell to persuade Tyndale to return to England to reinforce the establishment of the Anglican Church, but Tyndale said he would return only if Henry sanctioned a Bible in English.

Chapter 1 of St John's Gospel by William Tyndale, 1522.

The most troublesome parts of Tyndale's translation, which were seen as heretical by the Catholic Church, were his use of the word 'congregation' to describe the body of the faithful, which gave no role to the Church, and his use of the word 'elder' to describe the role of the priest, which again denied the special position of the clergy. Also heretical was Tyndale's belief that sinners did not have to undertake penance for their sins through the sacraments of the Church: all that was needed was for them to repent.

Justification by faith was a concept that was to create a revolution which challenged the central authority of the Church and the power of the clergy. Ordinary people – at least those who could read – could now make up their own minds, or in Tyndale's own words, expressed to a group of priests before he left England, his purpose was to 'cause a boy that driveth the plough to know more of the Scripture than thou doest'.

Tyndale produced one of the major founding works of the English language, for about 85 percent of the famous King James Bible of 1611 was Tyndale's. His language was simple and at times monosyllabic so that simple people could grasp it – 'The Word was with God and the Word was God'; 'Under the sun'; 'Let there be light'; 'Pour out one's heart'; 'the apple of his eye'; 'fall flat on his face'; 'eat, drink and be merry'; and 'Our Father which art in Heaven' are memorable phrases that people could remember, repeat and cherish.

Cuthbert Tunstall was so appalled by Tyndale's Bible that he ordered all the copies in London to be bought and on 26 October 1526 had 6,000 Bibles burnt on the steps of St Paul's. He also redoubled his efforts to destroy as many copies as he could by getting an English merchant in Antwerp, Augustine Packington, to buy copies as they came off the press in the Low Countries. Tyndale rather welcomed this, as he took the money and arranged for even more editions to be published. However, Tunstall's destruction was remarkably effective, since only one copy of Tyndale's Bible has survived and it is in a library in Stuttgart.

The Catholic Church continued to pursue Tyndale and in 1535 he was betrayed to the officers of the Holy Roman Emperor, Charles V, by an Englishman, who had befriended him in Antwerp but who was a passionate Catholic. Eighteen months later on 6 October 1536 Tyndale was burnt at the stake, uttering his last words, 'O Lord, ope the King of England's eyes'. This dying wish was fulfilled, for in that very same year Henry VIII agreed to publish a Bible in English which was Coverdale's translation, but the one to survive was Tyndale's.

William Tyndale's death at the stake, 6 October 1536.

The Martyrdome of Master William Tindall in Flanders, by Vilvord Castle.

Lord ope the King of Englands eyes.

MICHAEL SERVETUS, UNITARIAN MARTYR (1511–1553)

Catholics were not alone in burning books and heretics. In the 1540s and 1550s Swiss and German Protestants persecuted and burnt heretics along with their books. Michael Servetus, born in Aragon and brought up by Dominican friars, at the age of fifteen studied law at Toulouse University and by nineteen was a page and secretary in

Michael Servetus, by Christian Friedrich Fritzsch, engraving.

the retinue of the Emperor Charles V, whose coronation in Bologna as the Holy Roman Emperor he had attended in 1530. Servetus was converted to Protestantism by witnessing the lavish luxury of the Pope and his attendants at the coronation.

He became a polymath and a leading figure in Renaissance Humanism, covering a wide range of subjects – Latin, Greek, Hebrew, maths, medicine, cartography, pharmacology and anatomy. At the age of twenty he published his first theological book, *On the Errors of the Trinity*, in which he expanded what was to become the central canon of his beliefs that the Trinity was not based on the Bible and that the real truth was the oneness of God, rather than a trinity of three distinct persons. This led him to distinguish Christ not as the eternal son of God but the son of the eternal God. This was the forerunner of Unitarianism and anathema to both Catholics and Calvinists. Apart from Servetus's religious writings he also published a study on pulmonary circulation which was the first to recognise that blood flowed from the heart to the lungs rather than the other way round.

In 1553 Servetus published *The Restoration of Christianity*, which took Calvinism head-on, rejecting the whole concept of pre-destination in which God condemned souls to Hell regardless of what they did or what they said. He asserted that God does not condemn men irrespective of their actions in this world – only a man can condemn himself by his own acts, ideas and expressions.

Servetus was then living in France under a *nom de plume* that he had adopted, Michael Villeneuve, but having been accused of heresy he was arrested by the Inquisition. Three days later he escaped but nonetheless he was tried in absentia and his effigy, together with his book, was burnt. He decided to flee to safety in Italy but made the mistake of passing through Geneva and even bigger mistake of attending a sermon by Calvin, where he was recognised and arrested. At his trial Servetus was accused of denying the Trinity and infant baptism. None of the leading Protestants, such as Luther or Melanchthon, were prepared to speak up for him and so he was condemned to death and burnt at the stake on 27 October along with what was believed to be the last copy of his book chained to his leg. However, it was discovered later that three copies had survived. In Calvinism also there was no space for freedom of expression or freedom of conscience.

The twisted logic of the fanatical religious bigot was clearly expressed by Calvin when he wrote:

'Whoever shall maintain that wrong is done to heretics and blasphemers in punishing them makes himself an accomplice in their crime and guilty as they are. There is no question here of man's authority; it is God who speaks and clear it is what law he will have kept in the church, even to the end of the world. Wherefore does he demand of us so extreme severity, if not to show us that due honour is not paid to him, so long as we set not his service above every human consideration, so that we spare not kin, nor blood of any and forget all humanity when the matter is to combat for His glory.'

This is the absolutism that has led bigots of all religions throughout centuries to justify the murder of those who dared to disagree with them.

'Whoever shall now contend that it is unjust to put heretics and blasphemers to death will knowingly and willingly incur their very guilt.'

JOHN CALVIN

THE MARIAN PERSECUTION

1553–1558

As soon as she became Queen of England and Scotland in 1553, Mary Tudor set about restoring Roman Catholicism as the religion of the country. Heretical Commissions were appointed to identify heretics – people of any rank or position who refused to accept the Pope as the Head of the Church or the real presence of Christ's body in the Communion. Across the country nonconformists, gospellers and conventiclers were hunted down; the Edwardine prayer book was burnt; and those who refused to adopt Catholicism were examined by special commissions and if they were still obstinate they were condemned to death by burning. Only a few recanted. These early Protestant martyrs were unbelievably brave, knowing full well that if they persisted in their belief they would be burnt at the stake. In the five years of Mary's reign 286 Protestants including fifty-six women were burnt.

Mary's first Proclamation of 18 August 1553 forbade the printing and selling of 'false fond books, ballads, rhymes and other lewd treatises in the English tongue concerning doctrine in matters now in question and controversy touching the high points and mysteries of Christian religion'. Other subsequent orders in 1554 and 1555 established an index of prohibited books and Justices of the Peace, mayors and sheriffs were ordered to search out such heretical books. In 1557 a campaign against heretical books was led by the Dean of St Paul's, Henry Cole, who was one of the most fanatical Catholics and who had actually preached the sermon at the burning of the former Archbishop of Canterbury, Thomas Cranmer. In 1558 a proclamation extended martial law to the search for heretical books and anyone found to have them could be summarily executed. This five-year Catholic campaign to stamp out Protestantism reached its peak in June 1557 when a nonconformist was burnt on each day of the month.

The persecution did not survive Mary's death in 1558 and it so happened that Cardinal Pole, her soulmate and passionate ally, died on the same day. The new Queen, Elizabeth, reasserted her supremacy as Head of the Church of England and within a year every bishop had been replaced, imprisoned or exiled and in Oxford all the college heads were changed.

In 1563 John Foxe published his book *Acts and Monuments*, which became known as *Foxe's Book of Martyrs*. It covered in great detail the numbers of those burnt in the Marian Persecution and its popularity made it the most influential book published in England during the sixteenth and seventeenth centuries. In 1570 the Convocation ordered that a copy of the book should be placed in every collegiate church. Foxe had researched his book well because many of those who had suffered were remarkably articulate, though it may well be that Foxe invented the famous last words of Bishops Ridley and Latimer, who were burnt together: Ridley said, 'Be of good heart, brother, for God will either assuage the fury of the flame or enable us to abide it.' Latimer replied, 'Be of good comfort for we shall this day light such a candle in England as I trust by God's grace shall never be put out.'

Martyrdom of Wolsey and Pygot, from Foxe's Book of Martyrs, c. 1703.

Bibles in English were consigned to the flames and Wolsey, a constable, and Pygot, a painter, both carried a Bible in their hands.

Burning of Martin Bucer and Paul Fagius, from Acts and Monuments *by John Foxe, 1563.*

Bibles in English were consigned to the flames and William Wolsey, a constable, and Robert Pygot, a painter, both carried a Bible in their hands.

It was not only books that were thrown on to the fires for on one celebrated occasion in Cambridge in 1557 the bodies of two dead Protestant theologians, Martin Bucer and Paul Fagius, were dug up, their remains put into two new coffins and then burnt. At the ceremony in the Cambridge marketplace the burning was accompanied by a two-hour sermon by the Bishop of Lincoln and the Blessed Sacrament was solemnly paraded through the streets. Cardinal Pole, Mary's great ally in the persecution of Protestants, had taken a personal interest in this event and had ensured that the veil, which covered the Sacrament had been blessed by Pope Paul IV. Cartloads of heretical books were also thrown on to the fire.

THE BOOK OF SPORTS

1641

When James I (James VI in Scotland), who had been brought up in Scotland by Presbyterians, succeeded Elizabeth I in 1603, the Puritans hoped that he would support their attempts to dismantle and even abandon many of the practices and customs of the Church of England. A Millenary Petition signed by 1,000 Puritans was presented to James asking him to ban the exchange of rings in marriage, the use of the Sign of the Cross in baptism and the clergy from wearing vestments. James rejected such changes but Puritanism reached across the country and provoked a number of local disputes, leading to one in Lancashire in 1617 when the Puritans sought to ban sports on Sunday, which they believed polluted the Sabbath and were a violation of the Fourth Commandment. When the Bishop of Chester asked the King for a ruling he approved the publication of *The Book of Sports* which laid down the sports that were permitted: archery, dancing,

Scene of iconoclasts from A sight of ye trans- actions of these latter yeares emblemized with ingraven plats, *1646, published by Thomas Jenner, engraving, British Library, London.*

'leaping, vaulting, or other such harmless recreation' together with 'May-games, Whitsun-ales and Morris dances and the setting up of May-Poles'. It also allowed 'women to have leave to carry rushes to the church for the decoration of it according to their old customs'. Only those who first attended church should engage in these sports, but bear- and bull-baiting and bowling were forbidden. The Puritans were appalled and called for the book to be banned.

In 1633 Charles I reissued the book with its original text, adding only Wakes and Ales (countryside festivals) to the list of sanctioned recreations, and he decreed that any minister who refused to read it would lose his position. This was an affront to the Puritans and William Pynne claimed quite falsely that Archbishop Laud had persuaded the King to republish it. After the Civil War broke out in 1642, the Puritan Parliament voted to resolve that *The Book of Sports* 'should be burnt at the site of the Cheapside Cross' and, for good measure, they also ordered images, crucifixes and 'Papistecall books in Somerset' to be burnt. A copy of the 1633 edition was offered for sale in 2012 and bore the inscription 'These bookes were burnt at London by Ye hand of ye common ha(ng)man by authority of ye Parliament 1641'.

VOLTAIRE (1694–1778)

By 1740 Voltaire had become one of the most prominent and popular authors in France – principally famous for his plays, which are now rarely performed. He had also built up an international reputation as a philosopher. Frederick the Great had long wanted Voltaire to go to Prussia and in July 1750 Voltaire accepted the post of Chamberlain and Poet-in-Residence, where one of his tasks was to try to improve Frederick's French prose and verse. He was able to dine alone with the King but this soon palled, as Frederick really looked upon Voltaire as a trophy intellectual.

This provided plenty of time to write and Voltaire soon became involved in a personal feud with Pierre Louis Moreau de Maupertuis, the French President of the Berlin Academy of Sciences and Belles-

Lettres. In December 1752 Voltaire could not resist publishing a vitriolic pamphlet that denounced and derided his opponent. This angered Frederick and he had the pamphlet seized and ceremoniously burnt by the public executioner. Voltaire wanted to leave but Frederick would not let him and so he published another pamphlet against Maupertuis in London, which led to his dismissal by the King in March 1753.

In 1764 Voltaire published in Geneva his *Dictionnaire philosophique portatif* ('Portable Philosophical Dictionary') which was very critical of the Catholic Church. It was published anonymously and he took a great deal of trouble to disguise his authorship. The book was widely condemned and burnt publicly in several European capitals, starting with Paris, but it proved to be very popular. A new edition was issued in 1765 with two further reprintings that year. A sixth, expanded edition in two volumes appeared in 1767 with

Frederick II of Prussia and Voltaire, porcelain, eighteenth century, French.

FREDERIC II ET VOLTAIRE

another two in 1769. It was an open secret that Voltaire was the author and the Genevan authorities brought a prosecution against the book. In September 1764 it was publicly lacerated and burnt by the public executioner. But Geneva did not want to let Voltaire go and he recorded, 'A magistrate came to ask me politely for permission to burn a certain *Portatif*. I said to him that his colleagues were the masters and why did they not burn me in person and that I had no interest in any *Portatif*.' Voltaire protested that at the age of seventy-one he was ill and almost blind and should not be persecuted. In 1765 the *Dictionnaire philosophique portatif* was burnt in Paris.

Voltaire took up several cases of miscarriages of justice, one of the most notable being the trial and execution in Abbeville in Normandy of the young Jean-François Le Febvre, Chevalier de la Barre. He had been charged with malicious damage to a crucifix, singing anti-religious songs and showing disrespect to a religious procession. The official charges were blasphemy and sacrilege. It was really more a case of high jinks by young men, but the figure of Christ had been defiled and a crucifix cut by a sword, so all the force of the Church and State descended upon this twenty-year-old man. In February 1766 the court found him guilty but as a nobleman he had the privilege of being beheaded. His companion, Jaillard d'Étallonde, was ordered to have his right hand cut off, his tongue torn out and to be burnt alive on a pyre. One of the damning pieces of evidence against Le Febvre was found when the authorities raided his room in the convent and discovered a number of books, including Voltaire's *Dictionnaire philosophique portatif*. The prosecution claimed Le Febvre had been incited to his crime by the corrupting influence of philosophy in general and by Voltaire's book in particular. Also sentenced was the *Dictionnaire philosophique portatif*, which was to be burnt on the same pyre as Le Febvre.

Voltaire was concerned about his own safety as a result of this case but he bravely took on a personal inquiry into the miscarriage of justice. The evidence against Le Febvre was fragmentary, rumour-based, unreliable and wholly insufficient. A local magistrate had whipped up the case because of a personal grudge against Le Febvre. Voltaire published a pamphlet on the case, for the death penalty had never been used as a punishment for blasphemy.

THE GORDON RIOTS – LORD MANSFIELD'S LIBRARY

Lord Mansfield's Library, 1780

'A metropolis in flames and a nation in ruins.'

WILLIAM COWPER

In the first week of June 1780 London was engulfed for seven days in a riot incited by Lord George Gordon, directed against Roman Catholics and those Protestants who had supported the Act repealing the restrictions upon Catholics owning land and educating their children in their religion. On Monday 2 June a mob of 60,000 led by Gordon crossed the river at Westminster and invaded the Houses of Parliament where they attacked peers and MPs. When the Lord Chief Justice, Mansfield, appeared the windows of his coach were broken, the doors beaten in and mud thrown in his face. Later the mob started to destroy and loot the houses of politicians and judges and after midnight 20,000 rioters descended upon Bloomsbury Square to attack Mansfield's house – tearing down its railings, smashing down the front door and throwing out into the square from Mansfield's library pictures, books, manuscripts and his robes of office – all of which were burnt. One book picked up by a rioter was a collection of letters from Alexander Pope and this seemed to prove Mansfield's involvement in Popish plots. The house was burnt down but Lord and Lady Mansfield had escaped and fled to their other house, Kenwood, in Hampstead. Ironically, Mansfield had not actively supported the Catholic Relief Bill, but the rioters were driven just as much by a 'levelling spirit against the upper classes'.

Mansfield's library of over 1,000 books contained several from Pope, Swift and Lord Bolingbroke, as well as his own notebooks in which he had made a record of the many cases over which he had presided, so this destruction was undoubtedly a major loss to legal history.

Mansfield's losses amounted to £30,000 including the library, valued at £10,000, roughly equivalent to £5 million in today's money. When the House of Commons offered to compensate him he graciously turned it down.

The poet William Cowper wrote:

And Murray sighs o'er Pope and Swift
And many a treasure more
The well-judged purchase and a gift
That graced his lettered store.

Their pages mangled burnt and torn,
The loss was his alone;
And ages yet to come shall mourn
The burning of his own.

Figures by Chelsea Waterworks observing the Fires of the Gordon Riots, 7 June 1780, Francis Swain.

Order was restored when George III intervened and ordered 17,000 troops to London, as the Lord Mayor had refused to read the Riot Act. Justice was swift – 210 rioters were killed by the troops and

twenty-five executed – two who had been identified as the looters of Mansfield's house were hanged in Bloomsbury Square just twenty-five yards from its ruins. In a debate in the Lords Mansfield defended the King's judgement saying, 'I have not consulted books; indeed, I have no books to consult.'

Mansfield was one of the greatest lawyers of the eighteenth century and he is commemorated in the House of Commons today by a life-size statue alongside those of Pitt and Fox. He had delivered the famous judgement in the Somerset case in 1772. James Somerset, a black slave, was to be taken back by his owner to be sold in Jamaica. In his judgement Mansfield said:

> 'The state of slavery is of such a nature that it is incapable of being introduced on any reason, moral or political; but only by positive law ... it is so odious that nothing can be suffered to support it.... I cannot say this is allowed or approved by the law of England; and therefore the black must be discharged.'

This was the opening act of the anti-slavery campaign, but it took some time to succeed – in 1807 the slave trade was abolished and in 1834 slavery was abolished.

A week later on the night of 8 June a mob stormed through Covent Garden, looting and burning any house it passed. One of its principal targets was the home and offices at 4 Bow Street of the blind magistrate Sir John Fielding. He had dealt severely with the petty criminals of this congested part of the city, using his Bow Street Runners to bring to his court criminals, thieves, pimps and prostitutes. He also started to keep records of the criminals – their names, addresses and length of sentences – so that previously convicted offenders could be given a harsher sentence. The mob burnt his house to the ground – doors, shutters, staircases, furniture and bed linen were thrown on to the fire, including all the criminal registers.

JAMES ANTHONY FROUDE (1818–1894)

1849

Froude was an eminent Victorian, one of the most well known and celebrated historians and biographers of Victorian England. He was famous for his twelve-volume history of England, which emphasised the role of the individual in instituting historical change and which expressed warm support for Imperialism. He is read by no one now and indeed you might well ask who has heard of him. He is, however, commemorated by a blue plaque in Onslow Gardens in South Kensington.

Froude had toyed with the idea of being a clergyman but he could not accept all the doctrines of the Anglican Church. In 1849 he published under a pseudonym *The Nemesis of Faith*, the story of a young man who entered the priesthood hoping it would consolidate his faith, but scepticism prevailed and, trapped by his parishioners

Froude by Linley Sambourne, for Punch's Fancy Portraits, 1882.

into exposing his doubts about the authority of the Bible and the existence of the Trinity, he resigned. Subsequently he had a passionate affair with a married woman, but in Victorian England that was an impossible situation, so they parted and he declined to a melancholy death.

The Nemesis of Faith was viciously reviewed, 'a manual of infidelity' according to the *Morning Herald*, and in Exeter College, Oxford, a copy was burnt by Mr W.J.W. Sewell, the Sub-Rector of the college, in the hall in front of the Fellows and the undergraduates. This destroyed Froude's career and he was forced to resign his Fellowship at Exeter. He also had to cancel the offer he had for a teaching job in Tasmania. His father, Archdeacon Froude, disowned him and he was treated as a pariah – the *Church and State Gazette* even suggested that the author should have been burnt rather than the book.

However, George Eliot and Harriet Martineau liked the work, but today it is only really of interest to those studying Victorian scepticism. Froude turned to his great friend, Carlyle, who gave him the good advice to be robust, 'Froude ought to consume his own smoke and not trouble other people's nostrils.' Carlyle appointed him his official biographer and in the life that he published after Carlyle's death, Froude, being a scrupulous historian, revealed the misery of the Carlyle marriage. Froude also instructed his executors to destroy all his papers.

Nearly fifty years after *The Nemesis of Faith* was published Froude was appointed the Regius Professor of History at Oxford.

THOMAS HARDY (1840–1928)

Jude the Obscure 1895

Hardy's final novel, *Jude the Obscure*, was published in serial form in *Harper's New Monthly* from December 1894 to November 1895, though he had been working on the novel from 1890. It is the bleak and depressing story of a young stonemason, Jude, whose ambition to go to Oxford is thwarted by the educational system and class snobbery. After his divorce from a vulgar and shrewish woman he eventually marries his cousin, who has rejected her husband. They live in grinding poverty and their two young children are murdered by a wizened little boy who then commits suicide. This drives them apart and Jude dies in a hovel in Oxford on the last Saturday of Eights Week, when the cheers and shouts of the students from the tow-path intermingle with the words of the Lord's Prayer that is being said over him.

Page of Jude the Obscure *by Thomas Hardy, ms. 1-1911, p. 1, c. 1894.*

This was the bleakest of all Victorian novels: it offered no hope and no redemption. The critics' comments were savage, as the very pillars of Victorian society were derided – marriage, Christian belief and the elitism of Oxford. *The Pall Mall Gazette* dubbed it *Jude the Obscene* and Hardy was offended by being called 'Hardy the Decadent', particularly when Ernest Dowson, Aubrey Beardsley, Oscar Wilde and Max Beerbohm were writing at the time for the *Yellow Book*, the flagship for the decadent movement. Hardy was particularly hurt by the comments of someone who he thought was a friend – Edmund Gosse – whose day job was working in the British Museum and who called the novel 'grimy' and went on, 'Mr Hardy concentrates his observation on the sordid and painful side of life and nature. We rise from the perusal of it stunned with a sense of the hollowness of existence.'

After she had read a draft of *Jude the Obscure*, Hardy's wife Emma did all she could to prevent its publication, as she was appalled at the sexual impropriety. It was immoral to her way of thinking and almost a degradation of her own position as a wife. In 1894 she went to London and begged Dr Richard Garnett, Keeper of Printed Books at the British Museum, to intercede and prevent publication, but he firmly rejected her request to intervene.

Hardy received a parcel from America which contained the ashes of the book and the Bishop of Wakefield, Bishop How, declared that he had thrown his copy on to the fire and went even further by getting the local MP to complain to Wakefield Council, which removed *Jude* from their libraries' shelves. Hardy was to refer to How as the 'miserable second class prelate' and later he said that if they had met then the Bishop 'would have found a man whose personal conduct, views of morality and of the vital facts of religion, had hardly differed from his own'.

This was the first time that a senior member of the established Church had actually attacked Hardy's pessimism so openly and even implied that he was an atheist. This was a charge that Hardy resolutely refuted. This hostile reaction to his latest novel was the tipping point in his preference for poetry. He had been writing poetry in the 1890s and now decided that verse was a safer and more effective medium to express his views about the world and humanity. He made this note in 1896:

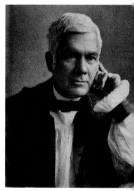

Bishop Walsham How of Wakefield, 1823-1897.

Poetry, perhaps expresses more fully in verse, ideas and emotions which run counter to the inert crystallised opinion – hard as a rock – which the vast body of men have vested interests in supporting. To cry out in a passionate poem that (for instance) the supreme mover or movers, the prime force or forces, must be either limited in power, unknowing or cruel – which is obvious enough and has been for centuries – will cause them merely a shake of the head; but to put it in argumentative prose will make them sneer or foam and set all literary contortionists jumping upon me, a harmless agnostic as if I were a clamorous atheist which in their crass illiteracy they seem to think is the same thing.... If Galileo had said in verse that the world moved the Inquisition might have left him alone.

H.G. WELLS (1866–1946)

The first Muslim Burning in Britain, 1938

In 1922 H.G. Wells published his *Short History of the World* in which he described the Prophet Muhammad as a 'man ... of considerable vanity, greed, cunning and self-deception' and he went on to challenge the divine authority of the Qur'an. As the Muslim community in Britain at that time was quite small, there was no immediate attack upon Wells and his views, but sixteen years later his book was translated into Hindustani and a reference to it in a local newspaper aroused protest meetings in Calcutta. This inspired in August 1938, at a meeting at King's Hall, Commercial Road, a Muslim organisation called Jamiat-ul-Musilmin affiliated to the East London Mosque to order that Wells's *Short History* should be 'ceremoniously committed to the flames by a party of Indian Mohammedans because of the reference to the Prophet Mohammed'.

This is the first recorded protest in Britain to protect the Prophet's reputation. There is no photograph of the burning but a group of East End working-class protesters, described in the *Manchester Guardian* as 'merchants, pedlars, clerks, sailors and others mostly from Poplar, some wearing the turban and some the fez', staged a march starting at Bank Station, down along Fleet Street to the Indian High Commission in Aldwych. The *Manchester Guardian*'s headline was 'Down with Wells!' and *The Times* said, 'Moslems' march through the City'.

Wells did not withdraw or apologise but sought refuge in saying, 'It is not fair to judge my views by a stray passage in an abridged version.' The Indian High Commissioner, Firoz Khan Noon, expressed his sympathy with the marchers and told them that he would hand their protest to the government, but that according to British law blasphemy was a crime only when the Christian religion was attacked. That argument was to be heard again when, in 1989, Salman Rushdie's *The Satanic Verses* was burnt by Muslim protesters in Bradford and when cartoons satirising the Prophet Muhammad were published in a Danish magazine/newspaper in 2005.

Jamiat's protest march against H.G. Wells's Short History of the World, 1938.

AMERICAN COMICS

1948–60

In the 1930s comic books came to be the most popular art-form in America. They sold in their millions for ten cents each and created such icons as Dick Tracy, Flash Gordon, Tarzan, Batman and Clark Kent/Superman. Detective stories were at their heart and that meant violence and sex, but the goodies won out at the end for 'Crime does not pay'. By the 1940s there were over 700 different titles each selling between 80 and 100 million copies, producing a revenue of $72 million. One even boasted on its banner headline that as comics were passed hand-to-hand it had five million readers. In the pre-television age readers liked their boisterous crudity, horror and romance, blazing guns, car chases, handsome heroes and scantily clad beauties.

The first attack on comics was in Wisconsin in 1940 by a journalist for the *Chicago Daily News* – 'the effect of these pulp-paper nightmares is that of a violent stimulant'. A 'pernicious generation' was being created and there were examples of children who had killed themselves re-enacting what they had seen in comics. The Roman Catholic Church put its weight behind this embryonic campaign.

In 1948 *Time* magazine carried an article on comic books entitled 'Puddles of Blood'. Psychiatrists claimed that juvenile delinquency was stimulated by an excess of 'pictorial beatings, shootings, stranglings, blood puddles and torturing-to-death'; and the magazine concluded, 'comic books not only inspire evil, but suggest a form for the evil to take'. Following this, local councils and police departments drew up a list of comics that should be banned or withdrawn from circulation – crime books were becoming criminal. In September 1948 the County of Los Angeles outlawed the sale of crime comics to minors.

The campaign that was to lead to the mass burning of comics started in the small town of Spencer, West Virginia, where most of the residents were farmers or miners. A teacher, Mabel Riddell, acting with the support of the Parent-Teacher Association, asked a bright pupil, one David Mace, to lead an uprising against comic books. He persuaded some of his classmates to join his crusade and they went from door to door collecting comics in milk crates. On 26 October 1948 they

piled 2,000 of them in the school grounds and, watched by the entire school of 600, David Mace took a matchbox from his pocket and lit a copy of the *Superman* comic. He had previously made a short speech, 'Believing comic books are mentally, physically and morally injurious to boys and girls, we propose to burn those in our possession.'

Burning comics, Spencer, West Virginia, 1948.

When news of this act spread, several Catholic parishes and schools decided to follow suit. One of the first was St Patrick's Academy in Binghamton, New York, where hundreds of comics – not those featuring Mickey Mouse or Donald Duck – were thrown on to the flames by pupils after the fire had been started by a nun. The whole school was paraded outside to watch it and they all sang a hymn – the Catholic Action Song. It was the children and students who were the prime movers, but local government across America joined in and the US Conference of Mayors produced a tenpage handbook, *Municipal Control of Objectionable Books*: so much for John Milton. Some State legislators drafted laws to establish a permanent censorship on comic books. The State Governor of New York, the Republican Thomas Dewey, who had failed the previous year to become president, vetoed the proposal.

The producers of the comic books reacted quickly, as they had seen the writing on the wall. They changed direction – dropping crime and instead focusing upon love stories and then horror.

Dr Frederic Wertham, a leading and respected scholar in psychiatry, published in 1954 a book, *Seduction of the Innocent,* which led parents to believe that Superman promoted fascism, Batman and Robin homosexuality and Wonder Woman sado-masochism. Politicians took up this cause and a witch-hunt swept across America. A wave of hysteria led not just to the banning of comics but to their burning, organised usually by head teachers and parents. The result was a publishers' code restricting comics, reducing their vitality and making them duller. Censorship once again won the day.

This censorship extended even to Britain when in 1955 an Act was passed, The Children and Young Persons (Harmful Publications) Act, which prohibited the sale or publication of 'horror comics' which portrayed 'violence, cruelty and incidents of a repulsive or horrible nature'.

JAMES JOYCE AND EDNA O'BRIEN

1914 and 1960

James Joyce and Edna O'Brien share the distinction of having their first book banned by the Irish Catholic Church. In 1914, Joyce's first book of short stories *Dubliners* and in 1960 Edna O'Brien's *The Country Girls* were denounced from the pulpit and destroyed. O'Brien's novel which frankly described the sexual life of two small-town girls scandalised the prevailing views of this strict Catholic society and it was burnt in Limerick, 'after the rosary one evening in the parish grounds at the request of the priest'.

O'Brien also recorded that her pious mother crossed out the offending words in her copy of the novel and placed it in an outhouse. These acts of blatant censorship had no effect on the sale of either book, nor did it discourage either of the authors to publish volume after volume.

SALMAN RUSHDIE (1947–)

1989

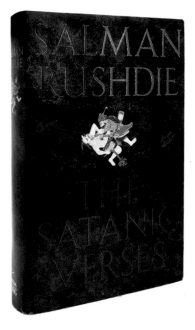

India was the first country to recognise that *The Satanic Verses* was a time bomb. An editorial adviser to Penguin, Kushwant Singh, told a magazine that 'there are several derogatory references to the Prophet and the Qur'an. Muhammad is made out to be a small-time impostor.' This did not deter Penguin from publishing the book in September 1988, but it disguised its interest by doing so under a different imprint. The Indian Prime Minister, Rajiv Gandhi, advised by an Opposition Muslim MP, ordered on 5 October 1988 that the book should be placed on its list of proscribed books.

Like most book-burners, the Muslim MP had not actually read *The Satanic Verses*, but that did not prevent him boasting of his ignorance: 'I do not need to wade through a filthy drain to know what filth is.' But he had been briefed by a Saudi-financed Islamist organisation, Jamaat-e-Islami, about the offensive passages – in particular the use of the word 'Mahound', meaning the Devil, which was a crusader's insult, and the depiction of the Prophet's wives as prostitutes. This body had branches in the UK with an HQ in Leicester, and a UK Action Committee on Islamic Affairs was set up to campaign against the book. It was not successful; Penguin went ahead and the British government pointed out that it did not ban books.

There were protest meetings and riots across the Muslim world and just forty-eight hours before the Ayatollah's fatwa seven people were killed in clashes in Islamabad and Kashmir. On Valentine's Day, 14 February 1990, the Ayatollah Khomeini dictated to his secretary a fatwa, the key sentence of which read:

> 'I inform all zealous Muslims of the world that the author
> of the book entitled *The Satanic Verses* – which has been
> compiled, printed and published in opposition to Islam,

the Prophet and the Qur'an – and all those involved in its publication who were aware of its contents are sentenced to death. I call on all zealous Muslims to execute them quickly; wherever they may find them so that no one would dare insult Islam again. Whoever is killed in this path will be regarded as a martyr.'

This incitement to murder was outrageous, because Rushdie had not committed a crime. Within hours the head of a charity in Tehran offered a reward of $3 million for his murder. For the ten years after the fatwa Rushdie become a fugitive, protected by four Special Branch police officers, not allowed to live in his own home, assuming a false name, Joseph Anton, drawn from two of his favourite writers – Joseph Conrad and Anton Chekhov – and constantly on the move. In desperation Rushdie agreed on Christmas Eve 1990 to meet six Muslim scholars in the safe haven of Paddington Police Station – the country's most secure police station. He explained he had no intention to offend the Prophet and he would re-embrace the faith he was born into. He followed this up with an article in *The Times*: 'Why I embrace Islam'.

'I am certainly not a good Muslim but I am able to say that I am a Muslim; in fact it is a source of happiness to say that I am now inside and a part of the community whose values have always been close to my heart.'

This was a completely futile volte face – Rushdie's liberal supporters felt betrayed and Muslims didn't really believe his recantation. Rushdie later admitted that this recantation was 'the biggest mistake of my life'.

Khomeini's fatwa was without precedent. Here was a religious leader in one country ordering Muslims anywhere in the world to commit murder anywhere in the world. Intolerance knew no boundaries – London, Paris and New York were no longer safe havens for writers who dared to criticise Islam. A worldwide de facto form of censorship had been established, as one of the things that the Ayatollah did know about was how to bully the world into silence. In Rushdie's autobiography, *Joseph Anton*, he describes how he became a hate figure for the whole Muslim world and how he 'had learned to withstand the Islamic attacks on him; after all it was not surprising that fanatics and bigots behaved like bigots and fanatics'.

On 14 January 1989 2,000 Muslims, both Sunni and Shia, marched through Bradford with *The Satanic Verses* fixed to a stake, where it was burnt outside a police station. The photographer Asadour Guzehan, commissioned by the *Sunday Times*, took the pictures that flashed around the world. Later he commented, 'There was a bit of a breeze and they had a few problems setting the book alight.... Afterwards I took some shots of the book, which were still intact but the pages were all blackened.' It is not easy to destroy a book by burning. In May 1989 20,000 Muslims marched from Parliament Square to Hyde Park in London and copies of the book were burnt on the way together with Rushdie's effigy. Tehran contributed $1 million to the demonstration.

In December 1989 7,000 Muslims marched again through Bolton in a rally organised by another Islamic faction, the Deobandis. Most of the Taliban leaders in Afghanistan in 1996 were trained in the Deobandi tradition.

Left: Muslims burning copies of The Satanic Verses *in front of Bradford City Hall, Bradford, UK, January 1989.*

Right: Anti-Salman Rushdie demonstration in Beirut, 1989.

Penguin, led by its chief executive, Peter Mayer, did not withdraw *The Satanic Verses* in spite of threats to staff and premises as a result of the fatwa. To their great credit, other publishing houses in London agreed collectively to publish a paperback version. In July 1991, the Japanese translator of *The Satanic Verses*, Professor Hitoshi Igarashi, was knifed to death on the campus of a university and in the same month the Italian translator, Ettore Capriolo, was beaten and stabbed in his Milan apartment. In 1993 Rushdie's publisher in Norway was shot but managed to survive. In 1993 in Turkey a mob surrounded the hotel where Aziz Mesin, the Turkish translator of *The Satanic Verses*, was speaking and demanded he should be given over to them to be murdered. The mob burnt the hotel, which led to the deaths of thirty-seven people.

This is a rather prophetic quotation from *The Satanic Verses*: 'A poet's work,' he answers. 'To name the unnameable, to point out frauds, to take sides, start arguments, shape the world and stop it from going to sleep. And if rivers of blood flow from the cuts his verses inflict, then they will nourish him.' THE SATANIC VERSES (PAGE 97)

The universal victim of the Rushdie fatwa has been free speech, as anyone since then who dares to write in any critical, disparaging or satirical way about Muhammad and Islam is bullied into silence. Few authors would dare to question the authority of some of the Prophet's declarations, which were recorded very many years after his death, or to say that Sharia Law has been created from later or questionable interpretations, and no publisher would willingly endanger their business, property or employees by publishing such a work.

Censorship over the ages has been sustained by groups of fanatics speaking for a minority but asserting that they represent the general will. The long hand of intolerance is relentless and unforgiving – Rushdie was banned from attending the Jaipur Literary Festival in 2012 and in 2013 the Chief Imam of Kolkata's Tupa Sultan Mosque applied direct pressure on the Chief Minister of Bengal to stop Rushdie attending the literary festival Kolkata Literary Meet – this in a state where Hindus are in the massive majority and which is also the centre of the great Bengali culture.

HARRY POTTER BY J.K. ROWLING

2001

The *Harry Potter* books by J.K. Rowling were burnt on 30 December 2001 at the Christ Community Church at Alamogordo in New Mexico. The Pastor, Jack Brock, who admitted he had not read any of the books, believed that youngsters were attracted to magic and witchcraft, rather than to their devotional studies, and he declared, 'The books are an abomination to God and me' and 'Harry Potter is the devil and is destroying people'. Many local people protested and one even dressed up as Adolf Hitler.

In 2003 *Harry Potter and the Goblet of Fire* was consigned to the flames at an evangelical church in Michigan.

Christ Community Church members enjoy a good, old-fashioned book-burning 30 December 2001.

OTHER AMERICAN BOOK BURNING

Several Pentecostal and evangelical churches in America have a penchant for book burning. Pastor Scott Breedlove of the Jesus Church in Cedar Rapids, Iowa, declared: 'It is part of our heritage. For centuries Christians have been making bonfires out of books and magazines that offend the sight of God. So why won't the city officials let us have a fire permit, so we can make a mighty conflagration outside our church?'

But the Pastor had met his match in the District Fire Chief for Linn County, Brad Brennerman:

> 'It is not a question of religious persecution. We simply do not want a situation where people are burning rubbish as a recreational fire. When we told Pastor Breedlove we would not grant him a permit to start a fire outside the Jesus Church, he said that we ought to at least allow him to hold a bonfire outside city limits. But that's not acceptable either, because County air pollution rules ban hauling material outside the city to burn it.'

Game, set and match to American officials. Breedlove had to make do with putting some books in trash cans and lighting a candle on them.

BURNING OF THE QUR'AN

2009

Yasuf is a village north of Jerusalem in the occupied West Bank, with both Jewish and Palestinian communities. In December 2009 an extremist Jewish group desecrated the village mosque and burnt over 100 books including the Qur'an and copies of the Hadith, the sayings of the Prophet Muhammad. The vandals also left a graffiti message in Hebrew that read, 'Price tag – greetings from Effi'. The 'price tag' is the settlers' policy of attacking Palestinian property, farms and even mosques in order to show their total hostility to the

Israeli government's decision, made after international pressure and President Obama's personal intervention, to freeze any new settlement building on the West Bank. The destruction of the mosques was condemned by the Israeli government, 'The torching of the Mosque in Yasuf is a despicable crime and the settlers are behaving with brutality', but that did not stop Palestinian youths stoning Israeli

The charred remains of a Qur'an were left in the mosque after the arson attack in Yasuf.

TIMBUKTU

2013

Following the French invasion of Mali in January 2013 and the recapture of Timbuktu, known as 'The City of 300 Saints', the Islamic Jihadists fled, but one of their last acts was to destroy many of the manuscripts and books held in the Ahmed Baba Institute. In their ten months' occupation of the capital, the Jihadists, apart from cutting off the hands and feet of blameless citizens and flogging women with camel-hide whips, destroyed 300 Sufi saints' shrines – an act comparable to the destruction in Afghanistan of the Buddhas of Bamiyan by the Taleban in 2001.

The literary heritage of Timbuktu stretches back to the fifteenth and sixteenth centuries, when books came south over the Sahara while gold and slaves moved north. In 1550 Leo Africanus recorded that in the busy market the richest traders were the booksellers. Libraries,

*Timbuktu,
29 January
2013.*

south of the Sahara, are rare and this one held Arabic manuscripts on astronomy, arithmetic, Islamic law and the mystic texts of Sufism. It was a rich legacy of Arabic learning and scholarship, as well as contemporary records of families, their poetry and the songs of North Africa sung in the local Fula language.

Fortunately, as the picture shows, the Jihadists burnt only some of the books. The most precious documents, manuscripts and books had been saved by the foresight of Abdul Kadir Haidera, a bibliophile and custodian of a vast library hoarded by his family since before anyone could remember. When the Tuaregs were seen in the city he bought as many metal boxes as he could and packed into them very carefully his private collection and then the most important items of the public collection. Then, with the help of a group of friends, they were carried out and 'we dug holes in the sand and buried boxes in the desert. There are also rooms with hollow walls, if you walked in you would never know you were standing in a room full of books.' This hero managed to save over 300 literary treasures.

PAKISTAN

2013

On 22 September 2013 there was an attack by two suicide bombers from the Taleban on All Saints Anglican Church in Peshawar that killed 127 worshippers and wounded another 170. In November a police officer guarding another church in Peshawar was shot dead. By preaching the words of the New Testament and by quoting from the Bible, Christians are accused under blasphemy laws, a tool for persecution whose penalty is death. In Lahore a neighbourhood called Joseph's Colony was burnt to the ground, with 200 Christians losing their homes. In this picture it is not only the cross that is being burnt, but the Bible, prayer books and hymn books which are being hurled into the flames of bigotry and intolerance. In March 2011 Shabaz Bhartti, the only Christian minister in the Pakistan government, was shot dead. His portfolio was Minister for Minorities.

Christian persecution in Joseph's Colony, Lahore.

WAR
BURNING

THE LIBRARY OF ALEXANDRIA

49BC, AD297 and AD642

The Library of Alexandria was founded in 300BC during the reigns of Ptolemy I and Ptolemy II, also known as Ptolemaeus Philadelphus, who were advised by a Greek, Demetrius Pholemis. It became a cultural centre for a community of poets, scholars, grammarians and historians who amassed a huge collection of manuscripts in Greek, Latin and Hebrew, including seventy-nine works by Aeschylus, 120 by Sophocles and ninety-nine by Euripides. An early catalogue ran to over 120 volumes. But it was a library beset and eventually ruined by a series of disasters and invasions. During the Egyptian civil war in 48BC, in which Julius Caesar supported Cleopatra, the two armies met in Alexandria, where Caesar launched an incendiary attack on the Egyptian fleet in the harbour and the flames spread to the library, destroying 40,000 books – a disaster.

Artist's impression of the ancient library of Alexandria.

After the conquest of Egypt in AD642 the General Amr ibn al-As asked Muhammad's second successor, Omar I, what he should do

with the books in the Alexandria library. The answer was lucidly destructive:

> 'With regards to the books you mention here is my answer. If the books contain the same doctrine as the Qur'an they are useless, because they merely repeat; if they are not in agreement with the doctrine of the Qur'an there is no reason to conserve them.'
>
> It was said that the rolls of papyri were used as a fuel for the public baths and that this lasted for months.

However, some scholars have argued that this account was an invention, propaganda by Christians, and others preferred to accuse the Romans of destroying the library in AD215, or Diocletian for doing so in AD297. There was also the probability of earthquakes, for between 320 and 1300 the area was subjected to twenty-three of these. Perhaps it was negligence, or possibly the governing authority at the time stopped funding the library in an austerity drive – a practice which has not entirely disappeared.

Moreover, in 391 the Coptic Pope, Theophilus, ordered the destruction of the Temple of Serapis which included the library, but there was no record of who the burners were nor what was burnt. The whole history of this famous library is enigmatic, speculative and full of myths, rumours and contested accounts.

CONSTANTINOPLE

The Fourth Crusade, 1204

The city that became the capital of the Byzantine Empire was founded by Constantine in AD330. It became a great centre for scholarship and learning and the Imperial Library contained copies of many classical texts – Plato, Aristotle, Herodotus, Thucydides and Archimedes – which ensured their survival. Up to the third century most texts had been written on papyrus, but parchment was then invented and this library was among the first to transfer its texts, while later, in the ninth and tenth centuries, they were transferred to paper. In the troubled history of the seventh and eighth centuries the Imperial Library was burnt on several occasions – in 781 hundreds of texts were lost and in 805 more than 120,000 books and manuscripts. The Byzantine Church also hunted down heretics, and in 1117 in its campaign against the Armenian Church it ordered the destruction of some of the works of St Cyril.

In 1202 Pope Innocent III called upon the countries of Europe to form an army for the Fourth Crusade, to recapture Jerusalem from the Turks. There was a thin response but eventually an army, principally of French soldiers, gathered in Venice, which agreed to provide fifty galleys to take them to the Holy Land on the condition that half their conquests should be given to Venice. The Doge of Venice, Dandolo, persuaded the leaders of the crusade, largely in the trading interests of Venice, to travel via Constantinople, where they could play a role in placing a new emperor on the throne who would pledge his support for their campaign in the Holy Land. The main interest of these Christian knights was plunder, pillage and looting. They laid siege to Constantinople in 1203 and in April 1204 the city fell to them.

The pillaging lasted for three days. What had begun as a Christian crusade was hijacked by soldiers of fortune, freebooters, land-grabbers and brigands with glamorous titles who diverted their wrath, lust and greed not against Muslim infidels but against a great city that had been the centre of Christian civilisation for nine centuries. The booty of paintings, statues, gold and silver plate, jewels, bronzes, carpets, precious furs and skins was divided among the victors – three-eighths to the crusaders, three-eighths to Venice and a quarter to the new emperor. The raiding was so comprehensive that Steven Runciman, the historian of the crusades, wrote, 'The Sack of Constantinople is unparalleled in history: there was never a greater crime against humanity than the Fourth Crusade.'

One of the great losses was the Imperial Library and a mass of documents from the ancient world, including most of the works of Callimachus, his *Hecale*, *Imbi* and *Aetia*. All that survived of his work were sixty epigrams and half a dozen hymns, and several of these were obscure and elusive. His most famous epigram, translated by William Cory in the nineteenth century, was:

They told me, Heraclitus, they told me you were dead,
They brought me bitter news to hear and bitter tears to shed.

Conquest of Constantinople from The Abbreviated Chronicle *by David Aubert, fifteenth century.*

It was not until the end of the twentieth century that papyrology was sufficiently developed to piece together the remains of tattered papyrus that had survived in the dry desert of Egypt. This resulted in the recreation of a quarter of the *Aetia*. So Bulgakov was proved to be right, 'Manuscripts don't burn'.

WASHINGTON

The Burning of the Capitol in Washington, 1814

When the British-American War broke out in 1812 President James Madison ordered the invasion of Canada. An American army reached Toronto and burnt the Parliament and its legislative library. Britain responded by advancing on Washington, from which the President had fled. On 24 August 1814 British troops set fire to the US Capitol and the embryonic Library of Congress, which had at that time 3,000 volumes and fifty-three maps, of which 700 had been bought in London. Once the war was over the Americans decided to rebuild the library and Thomas Jefferson had the cheek to suggest that they could buy his library of some 487 volumes, valued at $23,950, which they did! This library has now become one of the greatest in the world.

Le Baiser de Judas, (The Judas Kiss) October 1814. The print is an attack on the British attempt to induce the French to abolish the slave trade, which was violently resisted.

LOUVAIN

1795, 1914, 1940

The University of Louvain in Belgium is one of Europe's oldest, built in 1426. It became an important centre of scholarship, stretching back to Erasmus and Jansen. Napoleon's army in 1795 occupied Louvain and sent 5,000 of its best volumes to Paris. Shortly after the start of World War I, on 14 August 1914, Louvain had already surrendered to the Germans, but a stray rifle shot from a window instigated a vicious act of reprisal. 1,500 houses were burnt, 200 people executed and the university razed to the ground. The destruction included incunabula and thousands of manuscripts. The Kaiser sent a message to Woodrow Wilson, 'Louvain has been chastised'.

The Times in an editorial on 29 August 1914 thundered:

The Germans have committed an atrocious act which will turn the hands of every civilised nation in the world against them. They have utterly destroyed the peaceful and historic old city of Louvain, the Oxford of Belgium.... Even the library of 70,000 volumes and priceless manuscripts was committed to the flames by the ruthless barbarians who have set forth to spread 'German culture" throughout the globe.

After the war, many countries including America sent books to Louvain and an American architect carved a stone on its façade: 'What German madness destroyed, An American gift restored.' This rankled with many local people but even more with the Germans. In the World War II they repeated their earlier brutality and on the night of 16 August 1940 destroyed the library with an artillery barrage –

The Sack of Louvain, August 1914.

over a million books were burnt. The German sense of guilt was so great that they blamed it on the retreating British.

Among the books that were burnt in this new destruction were 200,000 that had been sent to the library by Germany as reparations for 1914, as the Treaty of Versailles had stipulated. Many of these books carried a bookplate:

Sedes sapientiae non evertetur
('The seats of wisdom shall not be overturned')

THE VINDICTIVE NAZI RETREATS

In September 1943, after the successful campaign in Sicily, a large force of Allied troops launched Operation Avalanche by landing at Salerno, just south of Naples, to begin the reconquest of Italy. In Naples, when a German soldier was shot by an Italian patriot in a street next to the Library of the Royal Society, a platoon of German soldiers marched to the library, sprinkled gasoline over the reading rooms and shelves, tossed in a grenade and then prevented firemen from approaching the burning structure. Over 200,000 manuscripts and books on the history of Naples were destroyed: so much for Germany's love of culture.

A group of British and American scholars, including the eminent archaeologist Sir Leonard Woolley, went to Italy to identify the most important works of art and cultural centres that had to be saved. They had the support of General Eisenhower, who issued an order decreeing that 'While in war men's lives count infinitely more and the buildings have to go... but in many cases the monuments can be spared without any detriment to operational needs.' The Allied troops were therefore alerted to do what they could to protect the ancient culture of Italy which the Nazis had looted and pillaged, sending back for Goering's personal collection many works of art and boxing up others in crates destined for later transport. They attempted to prevent these falling into the hands of the Allies by ordering that they should be stored in the Vatican.

On 30 September in Nola, a town close to Pompeii, German troops, following the command of their officer, set fire to a villa that was storing the contents of the Filangieri Museum and the state archives of Naples. Paintings by Van Eyck, Botticelli and Del Sarto went up in flames. Among the books that were burnt were 85,000 archival documents, some dating from 1239, the archives of the ruling Bourbon and Farnese families and the archives of the Order of Malta – it was thought to be the richest collection in Italy, second only to the Vatican's.

As the Germans retreated up through Italy they destroyed many artistic and cultural objects, including libraries. On the walls of one town they painted:

Chi entra dopo di noi non troverà nulla
('Whoever comes after us will find nothing')

If Past
Performance is
Any Criterion,
*cartoon by
Borman H.
Smith
(1892–1956).*

Similar acts occurred when the Nazis began to retreat in 1944, vindictively torching the Public Archives in Poland, Dieppe and Minsk.

As the Germans retreated to the north they took with them as much as they could, including works by Michelangelo and Donatello and, particularly paintings by Cranach, a favourite of the Führer, but what they couldn't carry they destroyed. Compared to the agony, suffering and deaths of many Italians the loss of libraries has to be seen as collateral damage – but nonetheless shocking, distressing and deplorable.

THE UNIVERSITY OF SARAJEVO

1992

During the break-up of Yugoslavia, Bosnia-Herzegovina declared its independence in March 1992. It was a multi-cultural state, with 31 percent Orthodox Christian Serbs (mainly farmers) and 44 percent Muslim Slavs (an educated urban elite). Within a week a Serbian army moved into Bosnia, claiming to recover the lands that had belonged to Serbia, and this launched a savage civil war, with the Bosnian capital, Sarajevo, under siege for three years. The Serbs were determined to destroy any Muslim records that showed Muslims living in Bosnia since the Middle Ages. On 15 August 1992 the Serbian leader, Milosovich, ordered the destruction of the National Library of Sarajevo.

The Serbs cut off the water supply around the library and shelled it with incendiary rockets and mortars while machine-guns kept citizens from removing books and held firemen at bay. The library contained 1.5 million volumes, 155,000 rare texts and 400,078 manuscripts: at least 80 percent were lost. One of the librarians said, 'There is nothing left here.' The fire lasted for three days and the Chief Librarian wrote:

> The sun was obscured by the smoke of books and all over
> the city sheets of burnt paper, fragile pages of grey ash,

floated down like dirty black snow. Catching a page you could feel its heat and for a moment read a fragment of text in a strange kind of black and grey negative, until, as the heat dissipated, the page melted to dust in your hand.

The author Valerijan Zugo said 'blackbirds' flew over the city for two days. The Serbs destroyed other libraries – Vinkovci, Vukovar, Zadar. The Bosnian Serb leader Radovan Karadžić claimed the Muslims 'took out all of the Muslim books, left the Christian ones inside and burnt Sarajevo down'. Once again fanatical and in this case ethnic bigotry attempted to distort history.

The plaque on The National Library in Sarajevo.

IRAQ: 'STUFF HAPPENS' – DONALD RUMSFELD

The Allied Invasion to Topple Saddam Hussein, Iraq War, 2003

Donald Rumsfeld, the American Secretary of Defence, at a press conference on 11 April 2003 commented on the looting of Baghdad in a phrase that has stuck in the public's memory:

> 'Stuff happens – And it's untidy and freedom's untidy and free people are free to make mistakes and commit crimes and do bad things.'

No hint of regret, or of responsibility, or even of apology. David Hare wrote a play on the Iraq War and used as its title '*Stuff Happens*'.

Rumsfeld was also responsible for the most famous quotation from the war – made before the invasion when there was no hard evidence of the existence of weapons of mass destruction:

> 'Reports that say something hasn't happened are always interesting to me, because as we know, there are known knowns; these are things we know we know. We also know there are known unknowns, that is to say we know there are things we do not know. But there are also unknown unknowns – the ones we don't know we didn't know. And if one looks through the history of our country and other free countries it is the latter category that tend to be the difficult ones.'

Rumsfeld left out a further category: 'What we do not like to know, namely that there were no weapons of mass destruction.'

On Wednesday 9 April 2003 Iraq's resistance in Baghdad ended as Saddam Hussein's statue was torn down. Just one month later on 10 May an international commission arrived in Iraq to evaluate the damage to the National library in Baghdad – Dar al-Kutub Wal-Watha'q. They discovered the Library had been looted twice and on the second occasion piles of books were amassed and burnt. The heat was so great that the Iraq National Archive was totally destroyed. Robert Fisk, the Middle East correspondent for the *Independent*, filed this report:

So yesterday was the burning of books. First came the looters, then the arsonists. It was the final chapter in the sacking of Baghdad. The National Library and Archives – a priceless treasure of Ottoman historical documents, including the old royal archives of Iraq – were turned to ashes in three thousand degrees of heat. Then the library of Qur'ans at the Ministry of Religious Endowment were set ablaze.

I saw the looters. One of them cursed me when I tried to reclaim a book of Islamic law from a boy of no more than ten. Amid the ashes of Iraqi history, I found a file blowing in the wind outside: pages of handwritten letters between the court of Sharif Hussein of Mecca, who started the Arab revolt against the Turks for Lawrence of Arabia and the Ottoman rulers of Baghdad.

A man stands near a pile of papers in the burned-out National Library in Bagdhad, 14 April 2003.

And the Americans did nothing. All over the filthy yard
they blew, letters of recommendation to the courts of Arabia,
demands for ammunition for troops, reports on the theft of
camels and attacks on pilgrims, all in delicate handwritten
Arabic script. I was holding in my hands the last Baghdad
vestiges of Iraq's written history. But for Iraq, this is Year
Zero; with the destruction of the antiquities in the Museum
of Archaeology on Saturday and the burning of the National
Archives and then the Koranic library, the cultural identity
of Iraq is being erased. Why? Who set these fires? For what
insane purpose is this heritage being destroyed?'

The American troops did not loot, but neither did they protect. This
was uniquely tragic, since Baghdad had been the cultural centre of
the Middle East.

CAIRO

2011

One of the most recent incidents of revolution leading to the burning
of books occurred in Cairo in December 2011. In what was called
'The Arab Spring' great crowds had gathered in Tahrir Square in the
centre of the city and occupied it until President Mubarak was forced
out of office. The transitional government, that assumed power to
guide Egypt towards democracy, was dominated by former officials
of the old regime, particularly the army, and the crowds began to
gather again in the square in the autumn. This time the army did
not stand aside, but moved to clear the square and the surrounding
streets, which led to ugly scenes of violence.

On 17 December a protester threw a Molotov cocktail through
the windows of Cairo's Institut d'Egypte, which housed 200,000
antique volumes and ancient manuscripts. Many of these had been
collected by the French scholars and artists who had accompanied
Napoleon's army of 50,000 men and 400 ships in the invasion of
1798. This was one of the oldest collections in Egypt and the Middle

East. The fire quickly spread throughout the building and destroyed 170,000 priceless documents of the ancient history of Egypt. The fire brigade could not get through because of the crowds and so some protesters and soldiers put themselves in great danger to pull out what they could, saving some 40,000 works.

Some of the unique and priceless books that were lost included the *Atlas of Lower and Upper Egypt* of 1752, the *Atlas of the Old Indian Arts* and the *Atlas Handler* of 1842, thought to be the only remaining copy in the world. The major loss was the scholarly work of French savants entitled *Description de l'Egypte*, published between 1809 and 1829. It contained everything they saw from Nile amphibians to the Rosetta Stone. It gave birth to Egyptology and the discovery of one of the oldest civilisations in the history of the world.

The Egyptian Minister of Antiquities claimed this was not a casual incident, but a deliberate act of desecration by saboteurs, who

Volunteers collect burnt manuscripts salvaged from the ruins of the Scientific Institute of Egypt near Tahrir Square in Cairo, December 20, 2011.

were seen on television setting fire to the ground floor of the Institut. Clearly the building was a prestigious symbol of the establishment and therefore a likely target when the frenzy of the mob boiled over. In retrospect one may ask why the government and the Institut were not more alert after the Arab Spring to the danger that their great library might have to face in the very centre of revolutionary events. During the Blitz in London in 1940 the directors of the British Museum had rather more foresight, as they moved the Rosetta Stone – which had been seized by the British after the overthrow of Napoleon's army in 1801 – to the depths of the underground.

On 14 August 2013, after the army had deposed the Morsi Government – successors to the overthrown Mubarak – and banned the Muslim Brotherhood, members of the Brotherhood decided to punish the new military-dominated government by raiding the Malawii Antiquities Museum, some 200 miles south of Cairo. In their eyes the museum was a manifestation of the government rather than the State of Egypt, as one witness recognised, 'It was a political act to get back at the State.' But other marauders, armed gangs and looters occupied the museum, taking out over 100 objects. Irreplaceable documents made from papyrus were stolen or destroyed. Objects such as mummies, which were too large to be taken, were burnt.

PERSONAL
BURNING

The Earl of
Rochester *by*
Jacob
Huysmans,
c. 1675.

Devouring time swallows us whole;
Impartial death confounds body and soul.
For Hell and the foul fiend that rules.

In the spring of 1680 Rochester left London to return to his country house at Woodstock, where he was to die, surrounded by his family – his mother, his wife and his children. Prudently he had sent back to France his handsome young valet who enjoyed the alluring name of Jean Baptiste de Belle Fasse, which advertised to the world he had 'Beautiful Buttocks'. Rochester told one of his friends that 'the greatest and bravest of this court of both sexes had tasted his beauties'. Both Belle Fasse and his wife were Catholics and as the Popish Plot led by Titus Oates was engulfing London, Rochester had been concerned that being a Catholic or a sodomite would lead to the gallows.

Rochester invited an ambitious clergyman, Gilbert Burnet, a fashionable confessor who had also set his sights on a bishopric, to meet him and talk together about his life and beliefs. Their several conversations were later published by Burnet in a book. Rochester held out the possibility that he would change his mind about religion and a deathbed conversion would be a step up the ladder for Burnet. While Rochester acknowledged that there was a 'Supreme Being', whether Nature or God, he argued that Heaven and Hell were mere 'rewards or punishments' and that religious worship was only the 'inventions of priests'. He remained firmly sceptical – Graham Greene's comment in his biography of Rochester was, 'If God appeared at the end it was the sudden secret appearance of a thief.'

Several divines including the Bishop of Oxford, the Rector of Lincoln College and a Dr Price of Magdalen College struggled to save Rochester's soul by persuading him to confess his sins and to repent. Collectively, as the inevitability of death drew nearer, they persuaded Rochester to become more contrite as he prepared to meet his maker. One piece of advice he gave to his son was that he hoped he might never be a wit.

It was Robert Parsons, his mother's chaplain, who achieved the libertine's miraculous *volte-face*. Rochester summoned his family to his deathbed to deliver his 'dying Remonstrance', which had been written by his formidable mother and signed by himself. 'From the bottom of my soul I detest and abhor the whole course of my former wicked life.' In his youth the 'lusts of the flesh, of the eye and the pride of life' had captivated him. *In extremis* Rochester ordered his relatives to burn all his 'profane and lewd Writings' and all his 'obscene and filthy Pictures'.

Much was lost. Rochester had previously asked his mother to burn his papers, among which were letters to Saville, an old friend from his Oxford days, which would have given a vivid picture of the Restoration court.

Horace Walpole later noted, 'Did I ever tell you a most admired *bon mot* of Mr Bentley? He was talking to me of an old Lady St John who burnt a whole trunk of letters of the famous Lord Rochester, "For which", said Mr Bentley, "her soul is now burning in Heaven".' But she could not destroy his poems. Someone had made a collection of his poetry manuscripts which was published within three months of his death as *Poems on Several Occasions*, and it was purportedly printed in Antwerp. Samuel Pepys bought a copy and kept it locked in a drawer, as it was written 'in a style I thought unfit to mix with my other books'.

The only poems by Rochester that appeared in the nineteenth century in a few anthologies were a handful of his beautiful songs. The rest were kept in the Private Case of the British Museum, to be seen only by scholars. Hazlitt admired him, but Dr Johnson dismissed him as 'worthless and useless – blazed out his youth and his health in lavish voluptuousness'. This was too harsh a verdict, for Rochester had certainly written one great poem, *Satire Against Reason and Mankind*, and some of the wittiest verses of the late seventeenth century.

In 1926 John Hayward published the first collected edition of Rochester and just escaped prosecution, because only 1,050 copies were published and these were offered to private subscribers. The New York customs destroyed all the copies that reached America.

Jonathan Swift
*by Charles
Jervas, 1710.*

JONATHAN SWIFT (1667–1745)

On Burning a Dull POEM
Written in the Year 1729

An Ass's Hoof alone can hold
That pois'nous Juice which kills by Cold.
Methought, when I this Poem read,
No Vessel but an Ass's Head,
Such frigid Fustian could contain;
I mean the Head without the Brain.
The cold Conceits, the chilling Thoughts,
Went down like stupefying Draughts:
I found my Head began to swim,
A Numbness crept through ev'ry Limb:
In Haste, with Imprecations dire,
I threw the Volume in the Fire:
When, who could think, tho' cold as Ice,
It burnt to Ashes in a Trice.

How could I more enhaunce its Fame?
Though born in Snow, it dy'd in Flame.

JONATHAN SWIFT

DR SAMUEL JOHNSON (1709–1784)

Boswell records:

> The consideration of the numerous papers of which he
> was possessed seems to have struck Johnson's mind with a
> sudden anxiety and as they were in great confusion it is much
> to be lamented that he had not entrusted some faithful and
> discreet person with the care and selection of them, instead

Dr Johnson *by*
James Barry,
c. 1778–80.

of which he, in a precipitant manner, burnt large masses of them, with little regard, as I apprehend, to discrimination.

Among these papers were 'two quarto volumes, containing a full, fair and most particular account of his own life, from Johnson's earliest recollections'. What a loss, for there may have been insights into his many eccentricities and even his 'black dog' – the bouts of melancholy to which he sometimes succumbed. Boswell knew about these volumes of autobiography, having dipped into them surreptitiously. Admitting this to Johnson, he was told that if he had absconded with the volumes, 'I believe I should have gone mad'. We will never know what made Johnson eventually burn the story of his life, but the loss was an even greater gain, for Boswell would have lost the opportunity to write one of the great biographies in the English language.

In 1784 Hester Thrale, Johnson's 'dear mistress' for sixteen years, became a widow when her brewer husband died. She then married her daughter's Roman Catholic music master, Signor Piozzi. Her children were appalled, her friends astonished and Dr Johnson was devastated. He returned to his house in London and burnt all her letters. His friends said it helped him to his grave.

CHARLES LAMB (1775–1835)

Charles Lamb met Samuel Taylor Coleridge when they were both at Christ's Hospital and a friendship developed which was to endure and to be one of the most stable relationships in Lamb's troubled life. Coleridge's poetic imagination and compelling personality inspired in this highly strung young boy, subject to fits of melancholy, a love of poetry and literature and especially plays.

Lamb's first published work was a poem in *The Morning Chronicle* in 1794 celebrating the performance of the great actress Mrs Siddons, which left him in tears. After school and after Coleridge had left Cambridge without a degree, their friendship flourished and they even planned to publish a joint volume of poetry, even

Charles Lamb
*by Henry
Meyer, 1826.*

though Lamb's poems were nowhere near as imaginative as those of Coleridge. There was a strain of hereditary madness in the Lamb family and Charles told Coleridge in a letter in 1796 that when he was twenty-one he had spent six weeks 'very agreeably in a madhouse in Hoxton … But Mad I was'. Lamb would move quite suddenly from very high spirits to morbid moments of melancholy, brought on through living with his father, who was becoming senile, and his mother, who was partially paralysed and whom his sister, Mary, had to nurse.

A dreadful tragedy was about to overtake the Lamb family. One afternoon in September 1796 Mary picked up a knife and stabbed her mother to death in front of Charles and her own father, who tried to restrain her. Within two days the coroner's jury gave their verdict of Lunacy and admitted Mary to an Islington madhouse. After this terrible calamity Lamb told Coleridge in a letter how much this had affected him:

'With me the former things have passed away and I have something more to do than to feel – God Almighty have us all in his keeping … mention nothing of poetry. I have destroyed every vestige of past vanities of that kind.'

From then on Charles's life was devoted to caring for his sister, sometimes in a private asylum, sometimes living with friends and sometimes just with him. This unselfish, loving care was a daily commitment which he was able to maintain only through his clerical job with the East India Company. One friend saw them quietly walking together on a melancholy journey to an asylum, both in tears.

Charles wanted to be a writer to add to his modest income and with the help of Mary published *Tales from Shakespeare*, which became a children's classic, still read a century later. From 1820 he contributed essays to a new periodical, *The London Magazine*, under the pseudonym Elia. These became very popular, for they were not polemical or dramatic studies but Lamb's own private and personal reflections on the world, half humorous, half pensive. He wrote a few more poems, but he is remembered as an essayist.

ELIZABETH FRY (1780–1845)

The Gurneys were merchant bankers in Norwich and were descended from leading Quakers. Elizabeth was the fourth daughter of a large family – she had eleven sisters and brothers and suffered in her youth from ill health and melancholia. She became much more interested in religion than her parents and at eighteen underwent a conversion – she 'felt there was a God'. From that moment her strong religious belief fashioned the rest of her life: she adopted the Quaker dress and speech, becoming a Quaker minister in 1812, devoting her life to philanthropy and helping others, and she became in time the leading prison reformer of the day.

From the early years she kept a series of journals that recorded the details of her life and spiritual progress. In the late 1820s she became aware that people would be interested in her life, which could serve as an example to others. She burnt all her journals from before 1797 – the year of her conversion – and also tore out pages or obliterated paragraphs of her later journals. One has no idea what was lost, for she had nothing to hide. She was happily married to a fellow Quaker banker and they had eleven children. She may well have recorded some of the anxieties of an adolescent girl which later she did not want the world to know about.

From the records she emerges as a highly intelligent, sensitive and intensely passionate young girl, apparently hampered by low self-esteem, but if that was the case she triumphed over her inadequacy in a quite remarkable way.

Opposite: (top left) Elizabeth Fry reading to female prisoners at Newgate; (top right) addressing a Quaker Meeting at Plaistow, Greater London; (below) her childhood home, Earlham Hall, Norwich. From The Quiver, *London, 1882.*

IN NEWGATE

EARLHAM HALL

ADDRESSING THE MEETING AT PLAISTOW

LORD BYRON (1788–1824)

1824

On 17 May 1824 the manuscript of Lord Byron's memoirs was burnt in the fireplace of his publisher, John Murray, in Albemarle Street, central London. Byron had intended that his two volumes of memoirs should be published, since he had shown them to his closest and most loyal friends, whom he called 'The Elect'. In 1819 he had given them, possibly as an act of charity, to his friend Thomas Moore, the Irish poet, who sold them two years later to Murray for 2,000 guineas. But strangely, Murray never read them himself. He asked Gifford, the editor of *The Quarterly*, to read them and his verdict was that they were 'only fit for the brothel'.

The memoirs must have covered Byron's ill-fated marriage, though his wife declined to read them as she did not wish to be associated with or held responsible for any decision about their fate. Byron's own comment was: 'the Life is a Memorandum not Confessions. I have left out all my loves (except in a general way) and many of the most important things (because I must not compromise other people) so that it is like the play of *Hamlet* – the part of Hamlet omitted by particular design.'

Six people gathered in Murray's office to decide what should be done about the manuscript. Murray and Hobhouse were for burning; Thomas Moore and Luttrell were for publishing; and the two representatives of Lady Byron, Wilmot Horton and Colonel Doyle, sided with Murray. But it was up to those two to apply the match, as the others were reluctant to do it. Furthermore, only two of the six had actually read the memoirs.

It is highly unlikely that Byron in his memoirs would have listed his paramours, for his object was not to titillate a salacious public with titbits of his own sexual behaviour. He spent the last years of his life fighting for the Greeks and he would have wanted to cast himself as the supporter of the underdog and the persecuted. He would want to be remembered as a hero and not a philanderer. Nonetheless the world is poorer for the burning; the memoirs would never have been dull, and the language would have captured Byron's swashbuckling vitality and his romantic aura.

Long after his death it emerged in 1869 that Byron's widow had told some friends that the great poet had committed incest with his half-sister, Augusta Leigh.

George Gordon
Byron, 6th Baron
Byron
by Richard Westall.

going to happen, for Tennyson seemed to be preoccupied with his old Cambridge friends and Emily had become concerned about whether Tennyson really embraced the Christian faith. This led to the end of their relationship. However, ten years later, in 1850, by which time he had become a famous poet, he decided to propose to Emily, who in the intervening years had not found a husband. This was to prove a happy marriage, with Emily taking over all their domestic and financial arrangements.

Tennyson biographers have tried to establish whether Tennyson had had any affairs or indeed any sexual experience before he married at forty-one. Most of his favourite poets of the early nineteenth century – Byron, Shelley, Keats – had had a number of affairs and their experience and passion were reflected in their poetry. Tennyson did indeed write poems about sexual passion. The Lady of Shalott dies from unrequited love for a handsome passing knight, Sir Lancelot, bewitched by his physical splendour, his coal-black curls and his strong male voice singing as he passes her window. In *The Idylls of the King* Arthur's court is destroyed by the adultery of his wife, Guinevere. In *The Moated Grange* Mariana reveals her sexual frustration as her lover will never come to her. Emily was determined that there should be no trace of her husband's feelings or actions before their marriage. All the records the couple could lay their hands on were destroyed.

Tennyson, seated with a book.
Photograph by Samuel Perkins Gilmore.

CHARLES DICKENS (1812–1870)

1860: 'The Misuse of the Private Letters of Public Men'

In 1860 Dickens, helped by his daughter, Mamie, who was to devote her life to looking after her father, collected all the letters he had received and put them on to a great bonfire in the garden of his house at Gad's Hill. Dickens could not, of course, have burnt the letters that he sent to hundreds of people. Most authors are keener to destroy the letters they have sent rather than the ones they have received, but Dickens was quite determined, saying, 'would to God every letter I had ever written was on that pile'.

Some four years later he was approached by a friend of Leech, the illustrator and cartoonist of *Punch* who had just died, to see whether he had kept any of Leech's letters. Dickens replied immediately:

Gad's Hill
Higham-by-Rochester
Kent.
Tuesday, December 20 1864.

My dear Sir – I am very much interested in your letter, for the love of our departed friend, for the promise it holds out of a good record of his life and work and for the remembrance of a very pathetic voice, which I heard at his grave.

There is not in my possession one single note of his writing. A year or two ago, shocked by the misuse of the private letters of public men, which I constantly observed, I destroyed a very large and very rare mass of correspondence. It was not done without pain, you may believe, but, the first reluctance conquered, I have steadily abided by my determination to keep no letters by me and to consign all such papers to the fire. I therefore fear that I can render you no help at all. All that I could tell you of Leech you know ....

Your reference to my books is truly gratifying to me and I hope this sad occasion may be the means of bringing us

into personal relations, which may not lessen your pleasure in them – Believe me, dear sir, very faithfully yours
    Charles Dickens

However, the recipient has but one half of any correspondence and already the other half – the letters that Dickens wrote – fills ten volumes.

Dickens defended his reputation determinedly and at times ferociously. In 1860 he wanted to ensure that no details should emerge of the relationship he had started two years earlier with a seventeen-year-old part-time actress, Ellen Ternan. He had fallen in love with her while they were rehearsing a play written by his friend Wilkie Collins, *The Frozen Deep*. This led to Dickens telling his wife their marriage was over and he told the world about this in a public letter that was cruel, partial and unfair. However, he did not want to let his loving public know of his infatuation, and accordingly he put in place the most elaborate arrangements to hide what he was doing – a house in another part of London, an alias when he went there, no appearances of them together and simply no mention of Ellen. So successful was this subterfuge that none of Dickens's biographers have been able to establish how intimate this relationship was. His deception had worked – little wonder that he wanted all letters sent to him to be burnt.

Dickens, with the help of the immensely wealthy Angela Burdett-Coutts, established in Shepherd's Bush in the 1840s a home for fallen women known as Urania Cottage. Its purpose was to redeem prostitutes, saving them from imprisonment or the workhouse. Dickens became absorbed in the running of this refuge – commenting upon the clothes of the inmates, their regime, their record – and he arranged for visits by a pet bishop. He also ensured that there was a well-stocked library and music lessons were given by one of his friends.

Dickens interviewed most of the inmates and passed his comments on to the manageress, Mrs Harriet Morson. He is supposed to have recorded the details of those interviews in a casebook which would have been fascinating, since Dickens was a natural reporter with a keen eye for illustrative detail and compassion for the suffering and

In the garden at Gad's Hill with two of his daughters, 1865. Mamie is sitting. misery of women who had sunk so low. But, alas, the casebook has disappeared and a recent historian of Urania Cottage, Jenny Hartley, has speculated that it could well have been thrown on the bonfire in Dickens's garden.

SIR RICHARD FRANCIS BURTON (1821–1890)

Richard Burton was a most talented Victorian whose exotic life was totally un-Victorian. His parents' nomadic life across Europe allowed him to become fluent in French, Italian, English and Latin, to which he added Arabic after a spell at Trinity College, Oxford, when that language was not taught there. His father bought him a commission in the Bombay army and he served in India for seven years. He became an experienced swordsman and was to write a book about this later in his life. He soon mastered Hindustani with the help of several Indian lovers and then added Gujarati and Marathi. He had a remarkable gift for picking up languages – Sindi, Persian, Punjabi, Armenian, Portuguese, Pashtu, Telugu, Toda and Turkish. This linguistic facility was put to good use in the Sind where, in native garb, he became a spy for General Napier, who had asked him to investigate three brothels in Karachi popular with British troops but which had only eunuchs and young boys. In disguise, Burton found out the services being offered and produced a scandalous report that was never published. That led to the closure of the brothels, but his enemies put it about that he had indulged in the services offered in those establishments.

In his early thirties Burton embarked on a new career exploring remote and unmapped parts of the world on expeditions funded by the Royal Geographical Society. The first was to Arabia disguised as Sheikh Abdullah, a wandering Sufi Dervish, practising medicine and on a pilgrimage to Mecca and Medina. On his return he published *A Personal Narrative of a Pilgrimage to Al-Madinah and Meccah* in three volumes, which was to make him famous. This was unlike previous travel books, since Burton did not write as an interested tourist but as someone who had lived in the communities he was visiting, travelling by camel, caravan and dhow. He went on to travel to many other places, including Somalia, to explore the slave trade, where he was scarred by a Somali spear; to Zanzibar and to Central Africa to seek the source of the White Nile; to West Africa and Dahomey. He claimed to have discovered Lake Tanganyika as the source of the Nile, but this was disputed by his fellow explorer Speke,

Burton, a.k.a. Sheikh Abdullah, from Burton's Personal Narrative of a Pilgrimage of Al-Madinah and Meccah, *1855.*

who claimed it was Lake Nyanza. This led to a very bitter dispute, resulting in Burton ending his official voyages of exploration.

After each journey Burton published a book – over twenty-five in all, quite apart from 100 articles. These vividly described his adventures, the way of life of the natives, their customs, religious and sexual practices, which covered marriage, polygamy, clitoridectomy, infibulation, eunuchism, circumcision, masturbation, transvestism, the length of male sexual organs, pederasty and homosexuality.

Sir Richard Francis Burton *by Ernest Edwards, albumen print, April 1865.*

In 1843 Burton married Isabel Arundell, who helped him to become a British Consul, serving first on the tiny island of Fernando Po, then in Brazil, Damascus and lastly from 1873 to 1890 as the British Consul at Trieste. The demands of the consulate in this quiet backwater allowed Burton to start a third career by translating the Indian and Arabic manuals of love-making – *The Kama Sutra* (1883), *The Perfumed Garden* (1884), *The Hindu Art of Love* (1885) and *The Book of the Thousand Nights and a Night* (1885–88). The latter ran to ten volumes and became a bestseller, earning Burton the substantial sum of 16,000 guineas: the most he had ever made. There was also a supplemental *Nights to the Book of the Thousand Nights* (1886–1888) which ran to six volumes; and *Priapeia or the Sportive Epigrams of Diverse Poets on Priapism* (1880) – this from the Latin.

Earlier English versions of these classics had been heavily censored, whereas Burton luxuriated in sensuous descriptions of lust and desire. He had to pretend they were printed in Benares instead of Stoke Newington, as the critics were savage. In the *Edinburgh Review* Burton was 'for the sewers' and another dismissed the books as 'the Ethics of Dirt'. Burton's target was the inhibited squeamishness of the age and the hypocrisy of the Victorians' refusal to recognise or discuss sexuality. He asserted defiantly, 'Mrs Grundy is beginning to roar: already I hear the fire of her. And I know her to be an arrant whore and tell her so and I don't give a damn for her.'

This outburst of eroticism was published in the decade of the 1880s, when several groups were seeking to impose a regime of moral rectitude led by William T. Stead of the *Pall Mall Gazette*, who called *The Arabian Nights* 'a revolting obscenity'. In 1875 the House of Commons had at last raised the age of consent to thirteen. The Criminal Law Amendment Act of 1885 suppressed brothels and in the same year Henri Labouchere MP successfully moved an amendment which introduced imprisonment for two years for any man found guilty of 'gross indecency with another male whether in public or private'. The climate of late Victorian England was robustly homophobic.

In the last two years of his life, Burton embarked upon a new series of explorations – those territories of sexual behaviour unrecognised by Victorian society and in particular male-to-male desire. He prepared another and even more explicit translation of *The Perfumed Garden* which he called *The Scented Garden*, with its infamous *Terminal Essay on Pederasts*. This mapped out a geographical area of the world which he dubbed the Sotadic Area, where pederasty was common.

At the time of his death Burton had just finished his translation, which ran to 1,200 pages, but his wife, a strict Catholic, decided not to further his wish to see it published and burnt it, together with his diaries and the voluminous notes and annotations. She felt she had to justify this and did so in a letter to *The Morning Post* in June 1891:

> I have now a terrible confession to make to the world [...] My husband had been collecting for fourteen years information and materials on *a certain subject*. His last volume of *The Supplemental Nights* had been finished and out on 13 November, 1888. He then gave himself up entirely to the writing of this book, which was called *The Scented Garden*, a translation from the Arabic. It treated of *a certain passion*. Do not let any one suppose for a moment that Richard Burton ever wrote a thing from the *impure* point of view. He dissected *a passion* from every point of view, as a doctor may dissect a body, showing its source, its origin, its evil and its good and its proper uses, as designed by Providence and Nature. *In private life* he was the most pure, the most refined and modest man that ever lived and he was so guileless himself that he could never be brought to believe that other men said or used things from any other standpoint. I, *as a woman*, think differently [...] Sorrowfully, reverently and in fear and trembling, I burnt sheet after sheet until the whole of the volumes were consumed.

This was indeed a terrible confession: Isabel Burton even went further and said that in a dream her husband had appeared to her, ordering her to burn his papers. She clearly did not want her husband's memory to be that of 'a certain passion', which she implied was so shocking that she as a Christian woman had difficulty in reading *The Scented Garden*. She was not even tempted by an offer of 6,000 guineas and in fact replied that she would not even accept six million guineas. In her will Isabel stipulated that everything she left should be burnt: her papers, his manuscripts, his unpublished works, his remnants. Only a few escaped the flames. They were burnt out of a sense of love. Much was lost – Burton's journals from 1870 to 1890, Isabel's own teenage diaries, their letters, his unfinished manuscripts on the lowlands of Brazil, North and Central South America, Syrian proverbs, notes on the history of the eunuch trade, translations of Ovid, and studies of polygamy.

Late Victorian England would have welcomed the news but not Ernest Dowson, the most celebrated poet of the 1890s, whose poems appeared regularly in the *Yellow Book* and who is remembered for his poem with its famous refrain, 'I have been faithful to you, Cynara, in my fashion.' He suffered from ill-health, fell out of fashion and died in poverty a few years later.

Against my Lady Burton:
On her burning the last writing of her dead husband

'To save his soul', whom narrowly she loved
She did this deed of everlasting shame,
For devil's laughter; and was soulless proved
Heaping dishonour on her scholar's name.
Her lean distrust awoke when he was dead;
Dead, hardly cold; whose life was worn away
In scholarship's high service; from his head
She lightly tore his ultimate crown of bay.
His masterpiece, the ripe fruit of his age,
In art's despite she gave the hungry flame;
Smiled at the death of each laborious page,
Which she read only by the light of shame.
Dying he trusted her: him dead she paid
Most womanly, destroying his life's prize:
So Judas decently his Lord betrayed
With deep dishonour wrought in love's disguise.
With deep dishonour, for her jealous heart
His whole life's work, with light excuse put by
For love of him, or haply, hating art.

If Love be this, let us curse Love and die.
Nay! Love forgive: could such a craven thing
Love anywhere? But let her name pass down
Dishonoured through the ages, who did fling
To the rank scented mob a sage's crown,
And offered Fame, Love, Honour, mincingly
To her one God – sterile Propriety!

ERNEST DOWSON

THOMAS HARDY (1840–1928)

The Notebooks

From his early twenties Thomas Hardy, using a pencil, recorded in a number of pocket-sized notebooks his observations on people and places, stories he had come across, conversations he had overheard, as well as sketches of domestic distress, verse fragments and phrases that appealed to him. They became valuable sources for some of his characters – their names and their foibles – as well as phrases in his poems.

The first illustration is the opening of a notebook called *Poetical Matter* which clearly states in Hardy's own hand that the book should be destroyed on his death. Sydney Carlyle Cockerell, his main executor, was scrupulous in destroying anything that he felt Hardy himself would have destroyed. In his diary of 14 December 1928 Cockerell records that he destroyed all the first drafts of the poems that appeared in Hardy's last collection, *Winter Words*. This notebook survived the Cockerell fire and was intended for the Hardy Museum in Dorchester. It was borrowed from a relation of Hardy's wife by Richard Purdy of York University to assist him in compiling the Hardy bibliography. It seems to have been lost somehow or somewhere after he had returned to London. Fortunately he had taken a microfilm of the notebook and that is what has survived.

The second illustration is one of the pages from another notebook saved from the flames. It contains a drawing by Hardy of his belief system – the architect in him is speaking. What he called the 'Prime

Force or Forces' (God?) is also called the 'Will', 'the Cause of Things', or the 'Invariable Antecedent'. Hardy was often accused of being an atheist but his response was to say that he did not know – finding agnosticism more comfortable and less confusing.

This note of 26 August is very revealing of Hardy's early sexual susceptibilities. It was written after he had left London because of his ill health and was recovering in Dorset, where he was trying to find a way to bring his literary interests to life. Lulworth Cove is a bay some ten miles east of Weymouth which he calls in *Far From the Madding Crowd* Lulwind Cove, where Sergeant Troy faked his own death by drowning. Hardy wrote his poem *The Maid of Keinton Mandeville* about a young woman who had sung in a concert in 1878, though it was not published until 1920 in *Late Lyrics and Earlier*.

> Aug 26. 1868. To Weymouth with Mary. Found it was W^th Races. To Lulworth by steamboat. A woman on the paddle-box steps: all laughter: then part illness + the remainder laughter. M. + I alighted at Lul^th Cove: she did not, but went back to Wey^th with the steamer. Saw her for the last time standing on deck as the boat moved off. White feather in hat, brown dress, Dorset dialect, Classic features, short upper lip. A woman I w^d. have married off hand, with probably disastrous results. (Combine her with the girl from Keinton Mandeville, &c, as "Women Seen".)
>
> (? 1880 — 1920.)
>
> A
> Prime Force or Forces (God?)
>
> B   C   D
> Beneficent   Neutral   Maleficent
> Force.   Force.   Force.
> (God?)
>
> Scheme of the universe

In his mid-seventies, when Hardy was preparing his autobiography, which was to appear after his death over his wife's name, *The Early Life of Thomas Hardy* and *The Later Years of Thomas Hardy*, he read through all his notebooks and then destroyed most of them. He left instructions to all his relations to destroy the rest immediately after his death.

But some survived, probably kept by Florence Emily Hardy, his widow, to assist her in completing the second volume. In his notebook *Memorandum I* he had written, 'This book is to be destroyed when my wife or executors have done using it for extracting any information as to the facts it records, it being left to their judgement if any should be made public. T.H.' So Hardy left a measure of discretion to his executors. But the main executor, Cockerell, who had earlier advised Hardy on the distribution of his manuscripts, came down on the side of destruction.

The Manuscripts

Hardy preserved most of the manuscripts of his novels with meticulous care. They ran to several hundred pages, each covered with his clear, precise script, though there were some pages in the hand of his first wife, Emma Gifford. Hardy had them bound in green or red leather and in 1911, on the advice of Sydney Cockerell, he gave them to a number of libraries and museums. Some of the lucky recipients were the British Museum (*Tess of the d'Urbervilles* and *The Dynasts*), the Fitzwilliam Museum (*Jude the Obscure*), Dorset County Museum (*The Mayor of Casterbridge*), Royal Library (*The Trumpet Major*), and in 1918 he sent *Far from the Madding Crowd* to the Red Cross sale at Christie's. But some he destroyed.

Hardy's first novel, *Desperate Remedies* (1871), had a poor reception and he destroyed the manuscript, which had been copied out by his future wife while he was living in lodgings in Weymouth. The manuscript of *The Hand of Ethelberta* (1876) seems to have been lost but when a fragment of it was discovered in 1918 he destroyed it. Hardy was very anxious about the record he was leaving behind and, being a perfectionist, he wanted his work to be seen in the best possible way. Handwritten duplicate copies, omitting much of the earlier working pages, were usually made by him and Emma.

When he was writing *A Laodicean* in 1881, while living in Tooting, Hardy fell ill and for the next five months he dictated the novel to his wife. He was not prepared to retain the manuscript in his wife's hand and he burnt it. When he abandoned writing novels in 1896 following the bitter attacks on *Jude the Obscure* (see page 109) and turned to writing poetry, his custom of preserving only the best was followed. He destroyed the earlier working drafts of his poems and kept only the fair copies.

The Letters and the Rest

Hardy spent a lot of time creating his own record of his life and one of his earliest destructions was after the death of his first wife, when he burnt the diaries that she had labelled 'What I think of my husband'. The biography that appeared after his death and was published by his second wife was largely written by him, as we have seen. The result is a highly selective, polished and censored story. Many original records were destroyed in his lifetime and, as Hardy approached eighty, the rate of destruction was stepped up. His last gardener, Bertie Stephens, recalled carrying baskets of letters and papers from the study into the garden at Max Gate – a task carefully supervised by Hardy's wife, Florence – with his comment that 'the world will never learn what went up in flames on that day'.

On 7 May 1919 Hardy wrote to Sir George Douglas, 'I have not been doing much – mainly destroying papers from the last thirty or forty years, & they raise ghosts.' In September of that year he declared, 'I have been occupied in the dismal work of destroying all sorts of papers which were absolutely of no use for any purpose, God's or Man.' In the 1920s Hardy had sent a memo to himself to make sure that he would not forget to 'continue to examine & destroy useless old MSS, entries in notebook & marks in printed books'. Cockerell,

Thomas Hardy with members of the cast of the Garrick Theatre's production of Tess of the d'Urbervilles, *6 December 1926. This is the only known picture of Hardy smiling.*

his literary executor, later recalled how he had spent 'a whole morning burning (by his instruction) notebooks by Thomas Hardy'.

In this way Hardy guarded his privacy and controlled others' perception of him – the cloak of privacy was opaque.

Philip Larkin's comment on Hardy's cleansing of the record was: 'The notion of strangers handling the materials of his life was wormwood to him.'

And what was destroyed? 'Evidence, plain and staggering, of what lay behind the anguish of both novels and poems.'

Hardy had himself commented upon the anguish of being too frank, too open, too explicit, or too confessional: 'If all hearts were open and all desires known – as they would be if people showed their souls – how many gaspings, sighings, clenched fists, knotted brows, broad grins and red eyes should we see in the market place.'

Thomas Hardy Burning Letters

Commonsense does it.
First, bed it down, then rake over
Dry grass, dry sticks: that's the knack –
You don't know there's a breeze
Till it snatches; not too tight, though,
Or the match won't take.
That's it.

Now the paper blackens,
Wrinkles like dead leaves, stains red
As the flames worm through.
It catches. And the heart blooms. Blooms,
And fails into smoke. The ash settles,
And you die as it dies, consumed.
There's only a pale film left, more delicate than petals.

They're all at it, gumbooted, sentinel,
Forking on weeds, trash, contents of attics.
You can see smoke standing up all over Wessex.

Here's a man
Has a face only the mirror knows,
Who's watched himself burn there
And outstared the horror.
His pitiless scorched lip twitches.
I wonder, is that for a word
The fire glowed through
Before the heart crumpled,
Or because he sees
Scholars, years after,
Scrabble for ash on their knees?

JEREMY HOOKER, LANDSCAPE OF THE DAYLIGHT MOON, 1979

ROBERT BROWNING (1812–1889)

1845–46

Robert Browning captured in 1855 by Dante Gabriel Rossetti.

On 10 January 1845 the thirty-two-year-old Robert Browning, living with his parents in New Cross, wrote to the thirty-eight-year-old Elizabeth Barrett, whom he had never met, who was living in her father's house in Wimpole Street, saying in the letter, 'I love your verses with all my heart … the great living poetry of yours … the fresh strange music, the affluent language and true new brave thought … I do, as I say, love these books with all my heart and I love you too.' He ended with 'Yours Ever Faithfully Robert Browning'.

Thus was launched one of the most celebrated elopements of the nineteenth century. Elizabeth Barrett suffered from consumption, spending most of her day on a couch in an airless room, occasionally sipping opium. She was in effect an invalid, prematurely aged, and rarely went out, becoming virtually a prisoner in her father's house, for he had forbidden all his children to marry and he ruled them with an iron will. This passion to control everything was clearly in the Barrett blood, for their fortune had been made in a West Indian slave plantation. Elizabeth was amazed to receive such a letter, but it started an almost daily correspondence for two years. On 20 May Elizabeth and Robert met for the first time when he called upon her in Wimpole Street. After this meeting he asked her to marry him and followed this up with a passionate letter declaring his love. This she rejected: 'If I disobey you, my dear friend … I do it not to displease you but to be in my own eyes and before God, a little more worthy, or less unworthy, of a generosity from which I would recoil by instinct … you remember – surely you do – that I am in the most exceptional of positions,' and she signed it, 'Your friend in grateful regard'.

Elizabeth could see no way of escaping from her father. Browning replied tenderly but robustly: 'Will you forgive me, or promise to remember for the future and be most considerate.' He admitted his inferiority to her as a poet and apologised for his 'over boisterousness' but begged for 'your friendship I am sure I have not lost'. She replied saying that they should forget this 'exquisite nonsense' and resume their friendship. He was invited to come round at 3pm the next Wednesday. She returned to him his offending letter and asked him to

Bronze hands of Robert and Elizabeth Barrett Browning, by Harriet Hosman, 1853.

burn it, which he did. However, a copy has survived. The burning was meant to be the end of the love affair, but the letter writing started it all again. Browning moved on to 'my own dearest love' and Elizabeth's Christmas present to him has the words, 'Love me for ever'.

Elizabeth's doctor told her she should winter in Pisa, but her father dismissed this with 'heaviest displeasure' and nothing came of it. Browning in the meantime had published one of his most popular collections of poems and began to plan an elopement, but even that took several months. It came to a head when Mr Barrett was proposing to move out of London while Wimpole Street was refurbished. Elizabeth knew that would make escape impossible, and so on Saturday 11 September 1846 she slipped out of her house and was married to Robert at 11am in Marylebone Church. They kept this a secret until the date of her father's move was known and Robert got tickets for a train journey to Southampton and places on a packet-boat to Le Havre. Elizabeth slipped out of her Wimpole Street prison on Saturday afternoon, 19 September 1846.

Browning, like Tennyson, wanted to cover his juvenile tracks. His father told a friend in 1843, 'He has destroyed all his early poems that ever came in his way, having a great aversion to the practice of many biographers in recording every trifling incident that fell their way.'

Even twenty years later Browning was still on the trail of his old papers when he wrote in 1866 to a friend, Mrs Frederick Lee Bridell-Fox:

> Indeed, I want to see and ask you a favour, – promised me by your Father two or three years ago: he had, or once had, – so he thought, a few utterly insignificant scraps of letters and verse written by me when a boy: if you find them, do – for old love's sake, – give them to me again! I used to write to Miss Flower when I was twelve or thirteen years old, – she had the vice of keeping every such contemptible thing (as she told me) – and, in consequence, whatever she thought to keep, Mr. Adams or some congenial spirit now inherits. I applied for my belongings, I seem to remember and got no answer: but if anything you can lay your hands on, it will come to me I know.

Sarah Flower had been the object of Browning's boyish love and she had obviously received many of his effusions.

R.L. STEVENSON (1850–1894)

The Strange Case of Dr Jekyll and Mr Hyde
Stevenson wrote this novella in about six weeks in the autumn of 1885. His stepson, Lloyd Osbourne, created a legend that Stevenson had written a draft in three days, after waking from a dream, but when Stevenson's wife, Fanny, Lloyd's mother, said that Stevenson had 'missed the allegory' her husband threw the draft into the fire. Lloyd was appalled: 'Imagine my feelings as we saw those precious pages, wrinkling and blackening and turning into flames.' Lloyd was a master of romance and this description added some authenticity to the legend. Reluctantly Stevenson, after reflecting on what Fanny had said, wrote it out again 'in about three days of feverish industry'.

The puzzling thing about this story is that two full drafts of this novella have survived.

A Burning Refused: W.E. Henley
The friendship of Henley and Stevenson began in Edinburgh in 1873 when they were both poor and living a bohemian life. They met in the hospital where Henley, who had lost one leg, was resisting the amputation of the other. This was a long and close friendship – many letters were exchanged and they co-operated in writing plays together. Stevenson told Henley: 'It was your maimed strength and masterfulness that begot Long John Silver in *Treasure Island* ... the idea of the maimed man ruling and dreaded by the sound was entirely taken from you.' Henley struggled to survive as a journalist and was most successful in editing the *Scots Observer*, a weekly literary journal, to which he attracted all the young emerging writers and poets of the day from Yeats to Kipling. It became known for its militant conservatism and the advocacy of imperialism, taking its tone very much from Henley whose most popular poem, *Invictus*, ended with the defiant declaration, 'I am the master of my fate ... I am the captain of my soul.'

Stevenson, in the meantime, had achieved fame and recognition with *Treasure Island* and *A Child's Garden of Verses*. Henley, waspish and irritable, had a gift for falling out. He came to resent Stevenson's wife, Fanny, who was eight years older than her husband and who had devoted her life to caring for him as his health deteriorated when consumption took hold. She shielded Stevenson from his old friends, many of whom, being heavy drinkers and smokers, disrupted his writing and threatened his health. The Scottish weather was slowly killing him and the couple tried to live in several places, Davos, Bournemouth and California. Finally in 1888 they chartered a yacht in San Francisco to sail to the South Seas. This provoked an outburst of Henley's resentment and jealousy at Stevenson's success and his departure from Britain's literary scene. In a letter to Stevenson he accused Fanny of plagiarising a story she had written for Scribner's Magazine from Katharine de Mattos, who was a cousin of Stevenson. Henley ended his letter with, 'Forgive this babble and take care of yourself and burn this letter.' Having spitefully slandered his friend's wife Henley knew full well that Stevenson would not follow this last instruction: it was the act of a coward and a bounder.

Robert Louis Stevenson and his wife *by John Singer Sargent, 1885.*

As anticipated, Stevenson did not burn the letter and replied in cold anger demanding a withdrawal, signing himself Robert Louis Stevenson. Henley initially ignored this but some months later when he wrote again he did not apologise or withdraw. Stevenson's innate generosity could not be suppressed and he wanted to rekindle the friendship with his old comrade, but Henley would not budge: his hostility festered.

Stevenson died in 1894 and when his first biography was published in 1901 Henley reviewed it in *The Pall Mall Gazette* with sustained vituperation. He called his old friend 'This Seraph in Chocolate, this Barley-Sugar effigy of a real man' and derided one of the most popular writers of the time for 'his vanity, affectation, unscrupulousness and condescension'.

So the letter that was not burnt provoked one of the nastiest posthumous attacks on a great literary figure.

RUDYARD KIPLING (1865–1936)

Kipling, who had burnt his parents' papers after their death in 1911, once declared that no one was going to make a monkey out of him after his death. To defend his privacy he burnt thousands of letters and forbade his sister and such friends as would listen to him to quote what he may have said or even written to them. After his death his wife, Carrie, burnt a mass of unpublished material and letters, some of which she actually bought back from their recipients. She also told her own executors to burn after her death forty-five volumes of a diary she had kept.

It was rumoured that some of the material she burnt included poems and writings that were anti-Semitic. In late Victorian and Edwardian England there was a current of anti-Semitism flowing just beneath the surface. One of the most hateful poems in the English language that Kipling wrote was *Gehazi*. This described Sir Rufus Isaacs, one of three Liberal ministers who had in 1912 allegedly bought shares in the Marconi company, having had inside knowledge of a pending contract. The ministers were cleared by a Parliamentary inquiry and three months later Isaacs became Lord Chief Justice

Cartoon of Kipling by Bert Thomas (1883–1966).

of England. It was this that inspired Kipling's *Gehazi*. Gehazi was Elisha's servant who deceitfully extracted a reward from Naaman, whom Elisha had cured of leprosy. When Elisha discovered the deceit, he cursed him with Naaman's leprosy.

Gehazi

When comest thou, Gehazi,
So reverend to behold,
In scarlet and in ermines
And chain of England's gold?
'From following after Naaman
To tell him all is well,
Whereby my zeal hath made me
A Judge in Israel.'

Well done, well done, Gehazi!
Stretch forth thy ready hand.
Thou barely 'scaped from judgement,
Take oath to judge the land
Unswayed by gift of money
Or privy bribe, more base,
Of knowledge which is profit
In any market-place.

Search out and probe, Gehazi,
As thou of all canst try,
The truthful, well-weighed answer
That tells the blacker lie –
The loud, uneasy virtue,
The answer feigned at will,
To overbear a witness
And make the Court keep still....

The leprosy of Naaman
On thee and all thy seed?
Stand up, stand up, Gehazi,
Draw close thy robe and go,
Gehazi, Judge in Israel,
A leper white as snow!

Kipling, however, had no truck with the Nazis. In 1933, the year of Hitler's rise to supreme power, which saw the burning of books in Berlin in May, Kipling told his publishers to remove from his book covers the good luck Hindu swastika symbol, which he felt was now 'defiled beyond redemption'.

Kipling bitterly resented the number of pirated editions of his works and in particular the publication of anything that he wrote for which the publisher had not received his express permission. He was particularly incensed at what happened in America and described these as 'thefts under American Copyright'. The Indian publisher A.H. Wheeler had printed and sold Kipling's paperback stories in the Indian Railway Library – *Soldiers Three*, *Wee Willie Winkie* and *Under the Deodars*. Wheeler believed he could publish in 1890 some of Kipling's articles that had first appeared in the newspapers for which he wrote – *The Civil and Military Gazette* and *The Allahabad Pioneer*. Accordingly Wheeler brought out a collection under the title of *The City of Dreadful Night and other sketches*. Kipling insisted that the copyright was his and very determinedly ordered the publisher to send the 3,000 copies 'to the paper mills and there destroyed'. A year later he demanded that the unapproved publication of *Letters of Marque*, a series of letters on travels through Rajputana, which had appeared in his regular newspapers, be destroyed – another 1,000 copies. However, some must have survived, as they appear from time to time in the salerooms and I have a copy.

SOMERSET MAUGHAM (1874–1965)

Somerset Maugham spent a good deal of time and care in polishing, explaining and enhancing his literary reputation and concealing his most private feelings. He published two memoirs, *The Summing Up* (1938) and *Writer's Notebook* (1949), but neither gave a real insight into his innermost feelings and his relationships with those who had been closest to him during his life. There was no mention of his bitterly unhappy and scarred marriage to Syrie and his devotion to his lover, Alan Searle. After Maugham had completed *Writer's Notebook* he burned fifteen volumes of his diaries.

Readers discovered from the memoirs a meticulous description of Maugham's style and approach to writing. He admitted he had no lyric gift, no striking use of metaphor or flights of poetic fancy, but 'on the other hand, I had an acute power of observation'. He was in fact a good reporter who described in clear terms what he saw. He was proud of his simple style, which others could find to be plain, flat and rather monkish. Enduring criticism by the intelligentsia did not prevent him – indeed it might well have goaded him – to describe himself as 'the greatest living writer of English'.

Some nasty cracks in Maugham's polished reputation appeared in his ninetieth year when his daughter, Liza, resisted in court his attempt to disinherit her in favour of Alan Searle. Maugham was forced to put his case in malicious memoirs published in the Sunday Express, *Looking Back*. It was a vicious attack upon Syrie as emotional, bitchy, shady in business matters – and while she was Liza's mother he was not her father. No publishing house agreed to publish this and Graham Greene hinted that his mind was going 'sick … senile and scandalous'. Maugham would have been a happier man if he had just basked in the success achieved by his capacity to write novels and short stories that became bestsellers, even though the literary world ignored them.

However, there might have been a grain of truth in what Maugham wrote in his 1964 attack. Syrie, the daughter of the philanthropist Thomas Barnardo, married another wealthy philanthropist, twice her age, the pharmacist Henry Wellcome, in 1901. This came to grief after

her affair in Panama with an American. Syrie then took up with Gordon Selfridge, who had just opened his store in Oxford Street. In 1911 she met Somerset Maugham, London's glamorous leading playwright, whose conversation 'flashed and sparkled like dry champagne'. In 1914 Syrie became pregnant and Wellcome filed for divorce, naming Maugham as co-respondent. Feeling trapped in a relationship that he really wanted to end, Maugham did the 'honourable thing' and married Syrie in 1917. But he had by then met in Flanders a young American, Gerald Haxton, who became his boyfriend.

Somerset Maugham and his wife Syrie, 1917.

Maugham and Syrie led separate lives, even to the extent of having separate doors to their house in the King's Road, Chelsea. Syrie became a very successful interior decorator, persuading her rich friends to adopt a minimalist style in which white was predominant, and which could well have had an effect on the 'big white set' that became Hollywood's favourite and led to her opening shops in Chicago and Los Angeles. Syrie was at the centre of celebrity London, designing rooms for Schiaparelli and Wallis Simpson. Maugham, no doubt a little envious, looked upon his wife's work as trivial, demeaning and a nauseous embarrassment. Once he crossed Baker Street to avoid passing her shop, with the bitchy comment 'she's almost certainly on her knees to an American millionairess trying to sell her a chamber pot'. Maugham and Syrie were divorced in 1929.

E.M. FORSTER (1879–1970)

By 1910, following the publication of his three great novels *Where Angels Fear to Tread*, *A Room with a View* and *Howards End*, Forster's reputation as a serious and important novelist had been established. In that year, however, he expressed frustration that all he could write about was 'the love of men for women and vice versa' when what he really wanted to do was to write about homosexual love. In 1913–14 he did just that in his novel, *Maurice*, which could not then be published; indeed, it had to wait until 1971, after his death. Then it met a rather cool reception for it was not up to the standard of his other novels, but Forster himself defended it on the grounds that it had to have a happy ending – the lovers had to remain in love for ever and ever.

As this avenue of imaginative fiction at the time was blocked, Forster set about writing what was to be his most famous and popular novel, *A Passage to India*, in 1924. As he was finishing that novel he returned from India after various sexual entanglements and burnt:

> Indecent writings, or as many as the fire will take…. They were written not to express myself but to excite myself and when – fifteen years back? – I began them, I had a feeling that I was doing something positively dangerous to my career as a novelist. I am not ashamed of them … it is just that they were a wrong channel for my pen.

Unfortunately for posterity, this burning did not unblock Forster's creative powers, since he never wrote another novel. The rest of his life was journalism, essays, criticism and some work for the radio.

E.M. Forster *by Jessica Dismorr.*

His search for happiness with a male lover started with an Egyptian tram conductor towards the end of World War I; indeed, Forster had admitted that he was looking for a young working-class man. Eventually in 1930 he found a young policeman, but the happiness he drew from that relationship also failed to release his creative powers.

Forster, an only child, had a very strange relationship with his mother, who thought little of his work and who excited during his life both affection and disgust. He recorded, 'Had I treated her with more firmness we would have both been happier.' After her death at the age of ninety he destroyed hundreds of her letters, though he delayed reading the twenty volumes of her diaries. Eventually when he did so he tore them up, together with his own letters to her. His record of this morbid and depressing relationship was contained in his own journals and twenty-eight diaries, including a "Locked Diary", which were eventually published in 2013 since he gave no direction to his executors as to their destruction. These are completely frank, revealing Forster's worries, his rages, his *bêtes noires*, his own homosexuality and his many affairs, which show him as a serial adulterer. It also includes a passage of self-disgust: 'Famous, wealthy, miserable, physically ugly – red nose enormous … face toad-like and pallid … stoop must be appalling … am surprised I don't repel more generally … I would powder my nose if I wasn't found out … loss of sexual power.'

Forster, unlike so many other writers, did not mind that one day all this would appear in print. He wrote in his diaries, 'the older one grows, the less one values secrecy perhaps, anyhow I think there is little of me I feel worthwhile to lock up.'

JAMES JOYCE (1882–1941)

Joyce's favourite sister was Margaret Alice 'Poppie' Joyce (1884–1964) and he returned from Trieste to Dublin to see her before she was about to leave Ireland to join an order of nuns, the Sisters of Mercy, in New Zealand, where she spent the rest of her life as Sister Gertrude. Just before her death she gave instructions, which one can be sure her Order carried out faithfully, to burn all her letters and photographs, including those from her brother.

One can only speculate as to what she would have made of *Ulysses* and *Finnegan's Wake*, but Joyce scholars have identified at least one passage of which Sister Gertrude may have been the source. *Finnegan's Wake* includes a *haka*, the war-like Maori chant made by the All-Black rugby team before their matches, and it appears like this in the book:

Let us propel us for the frey of the fray! Us, us, beraddy!
Ko Niutirenis hauru leish! A lala! Ko Niutirenis haururu

laleish! Ala lala! The Wulingthund strum is breaking. The sound of maormaoring. The Wullingthund strum waxes fuercilier. The whackawhacks of the strum. Katu te ihis ihis! Katu te wana wana! The strength of the rawshorn generand is known throughout the world. Let us sau if we may what weeny wunkeleen can do.

    Au! Au! Aue! Ha! Heish! A lala!

This is very close to the *haka* written for the All-Black tour of Europe in 1924–5 and which was chanted before their match in Paris on 11 January 1925. Joyce was in Paris at that time but as he was having trouble with his eyes and considering an operation, it was most unlikely that he went to the match. In the Catholic newspaper *The New Zealand Tablet*, Gertrude's obituary, which was clearly written by a fellow nun, said that Joyce had asked her to send him the *haka* and its translation. Joyce had kept in touch with his sister and we shall never know if he had asked her for anything else that may have appeared in his books.

Sylvia Beach and James Joyce, c. 1922.

D.H. LAWRENCE (1885–1930)

This determined and proud lady, braving the snow, made her solitary protest outside Jim Haynes's paperback shop in Edinburgh, photograph by Alan Daiches.

Lady Chatterley's Lover was printed privately in Italy in 1928. The Obscene Publications Act stopped copies being sold in England and any that were found could be seized by Customs or the Home Office. Censorship was extensive: between 1950 and 1953 4,000 books were deemed to be obscene and in 1955 a Soho bookseller was given two months in jail for selling a copy of *Lady Chatterley's Lover*. In 1959 a Labour backbencher, Roy Jenkins, introduced a Bill to allow publishers the defence against prosecution if the book had 'literary

merit'. Although it was a Private Member's Bill it passed through both Houses that year.

In 1960 Penguin Books decided to publish *Lady Chatterley's Lover* at 3s 6d and sold 200,000 copies on the first day. The government decided to prosecute Penguin for obscenity and that led to a six-day trial during which leading writers like E.M. Forster, Rebecca West and Richard Hoggart defended the publication. Reports of the trial were front-page news every day. The leading prosecutor for the government was Mervyn Griffith-Jones, who astonished the jury and became a figure of ridicule when he asked them in his opening remarks whether this was a book which 'you will wish your wife or your servants to read'. The jury found for Penguin and in the following year two million copies were sold.

T.S. ELIOT (1888–1965)

After the death of his first wife, T.S. Eliot had a mistress, Emily Hale. Her letters to him found their way into the archive of Faber, the publishers. One day Eliot, who worked at Faber's, summoned the Keeper of the Archive, Peter du Sautoy, to his office and instructed him to burn Hale's letters. Du Sautoy, who had been the Chief Education Officer in Oxfordshire and came therefore from a background that lived by order, considered it his duty to fulfil this request, which he did.

Eliot also told a friend that 'If I could destroy every letter I have written in my life I would do so before I die. I should like to leave as little biography as possible.' He didn't try very hard, since this ambition was revealed in a letter contained in the fifth volume of his correspondence which covered only 1930–31.

ALLEN LANE (1902–1970)

The Penguin Book of Siné's Cartoons

The Burning of *Massacre*, 1966

In 1966 the Chief Executive of Penguin Books, Tony Godwin, decided to revive the tradition of publishing collections of cartoons, and selected the iconoclastic French cartoonist Siné for a collection to be published under the title *Massacre*. This was warmly supported by John Mortimer, A.J.P. Taylor and Malcolm Muggeridge, but the

Most valuable and most rare of all Penguin's publications.

DESSIN MORD-BIDE

L'Express published what Siné considered to be offensively reactionary article. As an inveterate *ami Algériens*, he felt bound to resign, and then set ab producing his own one-man satirical review, S *Massacre*, whose stark ferocity makes *Punch* an *New Yorker* read like *Little Women*, and even *Priv Eye* seem to have been edited by Godfrey Winn. S *Massacre* is, in my opinion, the high point of his work far, and has been drawn on lavishly in this volume.

The Fifth Republic is far from being a comforta place for the political cartoonist. Poking fun at Presid de Gaulle, as numerous writers and artists have disc ered to their cost, can have uncomfortable consequenc *Lèse-majesté* is as applicable today as it was in the ti of the Bourbons. Siné gets out of the difficulty brillian by being able to suggest de Gaulle unmistakably withc actually drawing him – just a little push outwards of stomach, a cubit to his stature, and, of course, the nc and there is Le Grand Charles to the life.

He uses this kind of shorthand a great deal and v effectively. His cartoons lack Low's majestic line. Th are not crazy compositions like André François's, exercises in poetic despair like Charles Addams's. does not offer, like Peter Arno, a gross representat f a gross age. Rather, he is a Gallic, de-sentimentali Thurber, whose art will, as I hope, find a wide circle dmirers and addicts in this country for its sharpn uickness and vividness; for the economy of the dr g, as well as a kind of photographic impressionism S es which is all his own – exact, and at the same ti rmless; like a mushroom cloud whose impend iversal *Massacre* provides the backdrop for his c ticular one.

Chairman and founder of Penguin, Allen Lane, found the book 'nauseating' and did all he could to stop it. The Editorial Board, although divided on its merits, agreed that it should be published. The book was greeted by a storm of protest alleging that it was blasphemous. The Revd Ernest Payne, of the Baptist Union, thought it was 'one of the most offensive books I have ever seen'. John Heffer, of the famous Cambridge booksellers, was 'horrified' and another celebrated bookseller in London, Una Dillon, told Lane 'for the first time in my life I have decided against stocking a Penguin'. *Private Eye* gloated over the dilemma of a staid figure of the publishing establishment trying to 'get with it' and predicted resignations.

Before publication Lane had suggested to Godwin that 'someone on the QT could pick up the copies in the warehouse and dispose of

them somewhere and report the book o/p [out of print]'. Godwin was shocked and nothing was done. This is what then happened, quoted from the history of *Penguin Special: The Life and Times of Allen Lane* by Jeremy Lewis (2005):

> Some time in December George Nicholls, who worked in the warehouse at Harmondsworth, was woken by a phone call at midnight and told to report for duty at once. Standing in the dark outside the warehouse were Lane, Mr Bosley (his chauffeur), Mr Singleton (his farm manager) and 'another person who shall be nameless' (but could have been Susanne Lepsius, though many in the office assumed it must have been Ron Blass). 'George, that bloody board outvoted me, but I'll have my own back on them,' Lane told Nicholls before asking him to open up the warehouse: he was after 'those bloody Sinés' and was determined to pinch the lot. 'Crikey!' Nicholls exclaimed – his account of his midnight adventure reads like a cross between *Beano* and an Ealing Comedy – but he dutifully opened up and the brown paper parcels of Siné were taken off the shelves, loaded into a van and driven away to Lane's farm: whether they were then burned or buried is a matter of debate. 'Now, we'll keep this a secret, we won't tell anybody, will we?' Lane told Nicholls as he prepared to drive off with his booty. 'You're the governor,' Nicholls replied. Next morning some 220 copies were found on the packing bench, overlooked the night before: Harry Paroissien took them away, declared the book out of print and told the warehouse manager to put any returns 'under lock and key'.

GRAHAM GREENE (1904–1991)

Vivien Dayrell-Browning so captivated Graham Greene when they met in 1925 that he was even prepared to abandon atheism and become a Catholic – a dilemma that was to run through so many of his novels. They married in 1927 and separated in 1948. Greene was very concerned in his later life that Vivien was going to write a book about their marriage, but she had come to realise that the interest of so many people in his life had become 'a burden around one's neck'. In the 1990s Viven burnt all of the letters she had written to Greene, though not the ones he had written to her. 'I didn't want other people to read them, they were personal. Now *his* letters – that's different: I kept all of his.'

The Italian writer Curzio Malaparte (1898–1957) moved from being a dedicated follower of Fascism, having joined Mussolini's march on Rome in 1922, to being a devoted follower of Marx in the 1940s.

Vivien and Graham Greene outside their home in Chipping Campden.

He settled in Capri and in his honour a book prize bearing his name was established. When the judges decided to offer the prize to one of his novels Graham Greene declined, on the grounds that in his earlier days Malaparte had urged Italians to 'burn the libraries and disperse the vile families of intellectuals'. Perhaps Greene would have been rather more forgiving if he had learnt that Malaparte's long journey of conversion ended with his becoming a Roman Catholic on his deathbed.

It has also been reported that Greene was so dissatisfied with his first book, *Babbling April,* which he was later to describe as an 'unwise publication', that whenever he came across a copy he destroyed it. *Babbling April* was a book of poems published by Blackwell in 1925, but most of the poems had previously appeared in small literary magazines, including two in 1923 in *Oxford Poetry.* The most revealing poem in the book was about Russian Roulette, to which Greene was to return later in an essay called *The Revolver in the Cupboard* – a potentially fatal flirting with death.

PHILIP LARKIN (1922–1985)

Larkin went to hospital for a few weeks in 1961 and while he was there he forbade his lover, Monica Jones, to go into his flat. Later he set out his reasons for this:

> 'I had left a few private papers and diaries lying around. Such things will have to be burned unread in the event of my death and I couldn't face anyone I thought had seen them, let alone been willing to expose you or anyone else to the embarrassment and even of no doubt the pain of reading what I had written.'

In this laconic and blunt sentence Larkin sets out the reason why famous or celebrated people are willing to burn their private papers – 'embarrassment' or 'pain'. But is the pain the pain of the reader or the pain of the author? Dull diaries record the daily routine of the writer but the interesting ones are full of barbed comments about friends and colleagues, or the espousal of provocative and extreme views and causes, which in the case of Larkin would have been sheer joy to read.

In the summer of 1985 Larkin succumbed to what was to be his final illness, and as December drew nearer he instructed his secretary, Betty Mackereth, who was his last love, 'to destroy my diaries'. Dutiful to the last, three days before he died, she shredded thirty volumes and for good measure she burnt the shredded strips of paper. She had no doubts: 'He was quite clear about it. He wanted them destroyed. I didn't read them as I put them into the machine, but I could not help seeing little bits and pieces. They were very unhappy. Desperate really.'

It is surprising that Larkin did not do this himself at an earlier stage during his last illness. Perhaps it was too much of a wrench to deliver into the flames each day, month and year of all the old memories, for they couldn't all have been gloomy. He was clearly concerned about his posthumous personal reputation, since his letters to Kingsley Amis, Robert Conquest and Blake Morrison were full of acerbic comments about other people and current events which could have led to him being described after his death, when he could no longer respond, as a racist, misogynist, bitchy, little Englander. He

Philip Larkin and Monica Jones, 1967.

would have been a fully paid up member of UKIP. He should have had greater confidence, since his posthumous reputation would rest on his poetry.

The destruction of Larkin's diary had been explicitly specified in his will but his instructions on his other unpublished work were confused and were held by lawyers to be 'repugnant' – the legal word for a deed that is self-contradictory. One of the clauses stipulated the destruction of all manuscripts, finished or not, but another allowed his executors the discretion of choosing which of his unpublished works should be printed. Larkin did not have too much time before his death in December 1985, since he had fallen ill only in the summer of that year. This meant that within three years of his death it was possible to publish his *Collected Poems*, many of which had not previously appeared in the public prints.

ALASTAIR REID (1926–2014)

Alastair Reid, the Scottish poet, translator and teacher, wrote his most famous poem, 'Scotland', in 1971 and it has been much anthologised since.

> It was a day peculiar to this piece of the planet,
> when the larks rose on long thin strings of singing
> and the air shifted with the shimmer of actual angels.
> Greenness entered the body. The grasses
> shivered with presences and sunlight
> stayed like a halo on hair and heather and hills.
> Walking into town, I saw, in a radiant raincoat,
> the woman from the fish-shop. 'What a day it is!'
> cried I, like a sunstruck madman.
> And what did she have to say for it?
> Her brow grew bleak, her ancestors raged in their graves
> as she spoke with their ancient misery:
> 'We'll pay for it, we'll pay for it, we'll pay for it!'

This poem was seen to express the doom of Scotland. The burst of pleasure which was experienced by the freshness and brightness of the weather in the hills is somewhat akin to Blake's 'Jerusalem' – there is a strong sense of hedonism in both. This is in direct conflict with the ancient misery of the Scots, the Calvinist gloom of the woman from the fish-shop in a raincoat who says, 'We'll pay for it.'

A poetry festival was held in the function room of the golf hotel in St Andrew's in 2007 at which a hundred Scottish poets were invited to read their poetry. Reid, who was then over eighty, was the doyen of the meeting, although he had lived a large part of his life outside Scotland in Greenwich Village, New York; Dominica; Spain; and for a time on a Thames houseboat, earning his living by translation and writing for the *New Yorker*. Some consider him to be the finest Scottish prose writer of his generation and a very gifted poet.

Reid was the last to speak. He had seen the lines of his poem 'Scotland' projected on to public buildings in St Andrew's during the week. I was then told by another Scottish poet, Rab Wilson, who was present, what happened next. Reid said that he was always asked to read the poem, which he did, but he called it a 'ball and chain round his neck'. He then drew from his breast pocket a piece of paper which was the original manuscript of the poem. He read it and then said, 'This is the last time I shall ever read this poem.' He took a lighter from his pocket, lit the paper and held it while it was burning. The audience of poets cheered and someone ran forward with a bucket to collect the ashes.

Alastair Reid in a bookshop in Wigtown, Dumfries and Galloway, Scotland, Britain, March 2009.

This is the only contemporary sketch of what he said.

TED HUGHES (1930–1998)

The manuscripts of Ted Hughes's poems are scattered all over the world. As a young man he sold them for £5 each to Bertram Rota, the London book dealer, passing on the proceeds to his wife, Sylvia Plath. However, when other collectors and dealers became interested, the price went up to £10 and even £20 and, realising their value, on one occasion Hughes bartered manuscripts for a chest of drawers. But, alas, some were destroyed. In 1961, when his marriage to Sylvia was beginning to fall apart, she became very suspicious one evening when Hughes was late returning from a meeting with a BBC producer. She tore up some of his manuscripts and even his copy of Shakespeare's plays that he had taken with him on their honeymoon. When shortly

Ted Hughes and Sylvia Plath in Concord, Massachusetts, in December 1959, shortly before moving to England.

afterwards she did discover his affair with Assia Wevill, Sylvia took Hughes's papers from the study of his house in Devon and burnt them in the vegetable garden. They separated in 1962.

Soon after Sylvia Plath's suicide Ted Hughes destroyed one of her journals to shield their children from her blunt comments. I also heard from one of his close friends that before Hughes died in 1998 he destroyed what remained of Sylvia Plath's diaries, letters and his own records of their relationship, not wanting such personal anguish to be pored over by millions.

The literary estate of Ted Hughes is very complex and is spread across the world. Hughes sold to the Emory University of Atlanta a large archive of his manuscripts before his death. In 2007 his selected letters appeared and then the British Library bought many items that had not been included in the Emory sale; other material appeared in Australia. Hughes's output was prolific and Jonathan Bate, who had been asked by Faber with the support of Hughes's widow, Carol, to write an official biography, worked exhaustively though most of the material, including a diary that Hughes had kept. Bate discovered that pages had been torn from it and clearly he had unearthed through his meticulous study some very interesting incidents in Hughes's life, but Carol Hughes decided to withdraw her cooperation from Bate's work. This meant that he could not quote directly from this material, as the estate controlled the copyright, even though it no longer owned the documents, and Faber would not publish. This did not stop Bate, who could make good use of paraphrase, and he has now published the biography with Collins.

———⊂∞⊃———

ACCIDENTAL
BURNING

THE LOSS OF GALEN'S WORKS – GALEN'S LOSS

AD192

Claudius Galenus, more generally known as Galen (130–210), was the most important authority in the ancient world on anatomical theory and medical practice, the creator of many surgical methods and the reservoir of knowledge which was recorded in books of medical remedies and cures. He had been born in the prosperous town of Pergamum in Asia Minor and, after his father had told him of a dream that his son should devote all his life to medicine, he decided to do so. He studied in

A bust of Galen, third century AD.

Greece and at the great medical school in Alexandria before becoming the physician to the gladiators in Rome, where he learnt a great deal about the treatment of wounds. He then became physician to Marcus Aurelius and saved the life of his son, Commodus. He recorded virtually everything he did and studied, which amounted to over 350 books – it was said that he employed twenty scribes. His work on drugs was the basis of medieval pharmacology and his analysis of the four humours that made up the human body survived until the seventeenth century.

One of Galen's letters came to light in 2005, *On the Avoidance of Grief*, which contained advice on how to cope with great personal disaster — but it also deals with the loss he himself suffered.

A huge warehouse, about the length of the façade of Buckingham Palace, had been constructed along the Sacred Way by the Emperor Domitian (AD81–96). It was called Horrea Piperataria – the 'Pepper Warehouse' – for Rome was the centre of the trade in spices from India, incense from Arabia and precious products from Egypt. This became Rome's most important commercial centre. Galen stored there most of his medical remedies, his records and some of his considerable wealth because in his own words, 'People were confident because there was no wood in these buildings other than the doors and these warehouses were not close to any substantial private homes. What is more, the facilities were watched over by a military guard.'

However, in AD192 in the reign of Commodus a great fire, which may have been started by lightning, destroyed first the Temple of Peace, Rome's most sacred building; the Temple of Vesta; and the Pepper Warehouse, as well as many other buildings, when the fire raged for days.

Galen lost all his records including the first copies of *On the Composition of Drugs According to Kind* and also his work in progress: 'I was soon engaged on research on some topics and I wrote a lot in connection with those studies. I was training myself in the solution of all sorts of medical and philosophical problems, but I lost most of this material in the Great Fire.' As a young physician Galen had collected records from the past and from other doctors. But there was a greater tragedy, as Galen records: 'Yet I have not mentioned the most terrible thing. For there was no hope of replacing my lost collection of books, for all the libraries on the Palatine Hill were burnt on that same day.'

JOHN STUART MILL (1806–1873)

Thomas Carlyle and the French Revolution, 1835

Thomas Carlyle had started to write his *History of the French Revolution* in 1834 and soon decided that it would require three volumes. He read extensively, and his friend John Stuart Mill sent him several books and offered to make notes on the manuscript which could serve as footnotes. The first volume was finished in February 1835 and the manuscript was sent to Mill to check. On 6 March Mill, utterly distraught, went to Carlyle's house to tell him that an appalling accident had occurred: the whole of the text of *The Bastille*, apart from four pages, had been mistaken by a maid either at his home or

John Stuart Mill, 1865.

at the house of his mistress, Harriet Taylor, for waste paper and had been burnt. That night Carlyle almost had a heart attack: five months' labour had 'vanished irrevocably; worse than it had ever been', but 'I can be angry with no one; for they that were concerned in it have far deeper sorrow than mine: it is surely the hand of Providence and by the blessing of Providence, I must struggle to take it as such.'

In March Carlyle completed the second volume and, undeterred, sent it to Mill to read. Then he set about rewriting the first volume, which took six months – 'the ugliest task ever set me', but he reassured a friend 'the burnt ashes have grown leaves after a sort'. Carlyle wanted to publish all three volumes together – the second being *The Constitution* and the third *The Guillotine*. He finished the third volume on New Year's Day 1837.

Carlyle's *History of the French Revolution* became immensely popular and established him as a major literary figure. It coloured the view of several generations. It is ironic that at various stages Carlyle described the force of fire and in talking of the Bastille he wrote, 'Let conflagration rage; of whatever is combustible'; the significance of the Revolution was to be 'the world-Phoenix, in fire consummation and fire creation in the Death-Birth of a World' and 'Sansculottism, rising up amid Tartarean smoke, many headed, fire-breathing and asking: "What think ye of me?"'

Carlyle's work remains one of the most vivid and compelling histories of the Revolution, which he saw as a destructive force capable of destroying everything:

> What then is this Thing called La Révolution which, like an Angel of Death, hangs over France, noyading, fusillading, fighting, gunboring, tanning human skins? La Révolution is but so many Alphabetic Letters: a thing nowhere to be laid hands on, to be clapt under lock and key: where is it? What is it? It is the Madness that dwells in the hearts of men.

Carlyle had a lot of trouble with his manuscripts. In his late twenties he had written a novel, *Wotton Reinfred*, but most of the manuscript was burnt in 1827. One of his clerks, Frederick Martin, stole part of the manuscript and published it after Carlyle's death.

In 1866 his wife, Jane Welsh Carlyle, died. Consumed with grief , he read her letters, which recorded her unhappiness, with a great deal of sarcasm and anger directed at him. Reportedly he had physically abused her. Nonetheless Carlyle faithfully collected all the letters and did not burn them, although he did say, 'I still mainly mean to burn this Book before my own departure, but feel that I shall always have a kind of grudge to do it.' But the letters were eventually published by Carlyle's official biographer, J.A. Froude (see also page 235), and exposed him as the bully of Cheyne Row.

THE BURNING OF PARLIAMENT

16 October 1834

The fire broke out when piles of wooden tally sticks, which were medieval duty tax records, were being burnt in the Palace of Westminster. In one of his London lectures Dickens recalled what happened: 'the stove overgorged with these preposterous sticks, set fire to the panelling. The panelling set fire to the House of Lords, the House of Lords set fire to the House of Commons: the two Houses were reduced to ashes.' By great good fortune the great oak hammerbeam roof of Westminster Hall did not catch fire as well.

The historian of the fire, Caroline Shelton, in *The Day Parliament Burned Down*, gives meticulous details of which records were burnt and which were saved, coming to the conclusion that this was 'one of the greatest archival disasters the United Kingdom has ever known'. Nearly all the Commons' parchments and papers were burnt, including the Committee Minute Books since the Glorious Revolution of 1688; Civil War records and pamphlets; details of all contested elections since 1736; a mass of petitions since 1607; and even papers going back to 1495.

At midnight the great antiquary Sir Thomas Phillips, whose own collection of early manuscripts rivalled that of Parliament, together with Mr Cooper, Secretary to the Record Commission, tried to save what they could. They organised volunteer salvage teams from the Clerks of the House and the Library Clerks and even some soldiers. On the upper floors, before the flames reached them, the rescuers bundled up records in curtains and threw them to the ground below, but fire hoses had turned this into a muddy waterway. Much was ruined by being soaked, soiled and trampled on, but what could be saved was then stored for safety in St Margaret's Church.

Seeing so much history disappear before his eyes, Phillips decided thereafter to house his own great collection in coffin-like boxes so that these could be readily and quickly moved if a fire broke out in his house.

The Lords' Library was lucky to escape the worst. One document of great historical significance that was saved was the Death Warrant of Charles I, signed and sealed by fifty-nine regicides including Oliver Cromwell. To display that today would materially affect its quality, and so a superb facsimile was made a few years ago and is now on permanent show in the Palace of Westminster.

The Destruction of the Houses of Lords and Commons by Fire on 16 October 1834 by William Heath, lithograph, 1834.

T.E. LAWRENCE (1888–1935)

On 25 March 1919 the self-made hero of the Arab Revolt, Lawrence of Arabia lost an early draft of *The Seven Pillars of Wisdom* when he left it in a black bag under a table in the refreshment room at Reading Station. He claimed it had been stolen, but one is never quite sure with Lawrence, for he did imply later to Basil Liddell Hart, the military historian, that he had allowed it to be lost – but to what purpose? Anyway, the manuscript was never discovered.

Lawrence then set about rewriting it from memory, as he had destroyed his original notes. This was a prodigious achievement, completed some time in the summer of 1920. One man, Colonel

T.E. Lawrence in Arab dress.

Dawnay, who had happened to read both texts, reported that one chapter that he had read more carefully than others in the original 'seems to be the same, word for word and almost comma for comma in the second version'. This second version was destroyed by Lawrence in 1922 'as it was the original and to be kept secret' and a third version was prepared in February 1922 from which eight copies were run off and printed on the presses of the *Oxford Times*.

Lawrence first went to the Levant in 1909, spending the next five years there. He started by going on a long walking tour of thirty-seven Crusader castles which he documented and photographed, but this record appeared in 1936, a year after his death. In 1910 he became an archaeologist and joined a British Museum excavation of a Hittite shrine in Syria; and there he learnt Arabic and met a young water-carrier, Dahoun, which resulted in the most intimate relationship of his life and may not have been sexual. Lawrence's dedication to the published edition of *Seven Pillars* was very personal:

> I loved you, so I drew these tides of men into my hands
> And wrote my will across the sky in stars
> To earn you freedom, the seven pillared worthy house,
> That your eyes might be shining for me
> When we came.

Lawrence also worked for the War Office surveying Southern Palestine. He acquired a deep knowledge of the desert terrain and the importance of the port of Aqaba, which was to be seized by the Armed Forces in 1917. He had written an early version of *The Seven Pillars of Wisdom* but as World War I approached he burnt this manuscript, probably in his parents' bungalow in Oxford in August 1914. So how this may have differed from the final version we will never know.

Lawrence's life is a series of enigmas, ranging from a period of wide self-publicity after the Great War, with many public appearances, often in Arab costume, depicting himself as the desert hero – Churchill was one of his fans – to be followed by a search for anonymity which he found by enrolling in the RAF as Aircraftman T. E. Shaw.

ROYAL
BURNING

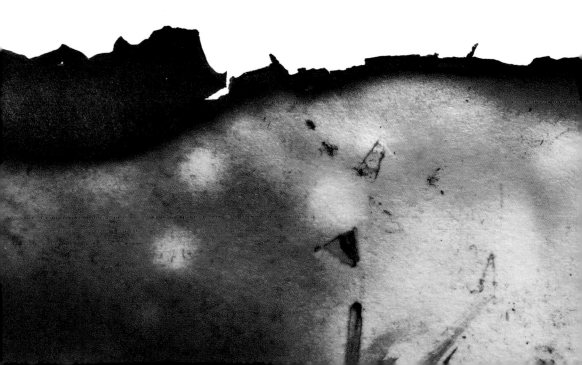

FREDERICK, PRINCE OF WALES (1707–1751)

Frederick was the son of George II and like many of the Hanoverian dynasty he fell out with his father. He established in Carlton House on The Mall an alternative court where members of the Opposition were welcomed. When in 1757 he died unexpectedly his wife, Augusta, ordered that any compromising political papers about Frederick's hostility to his father, particularly those in his own handwriting, be brought to Carlton House, where she would burn them.

CAROLINE, PRINCESS OF WALES, AND SPENCER PERCEVAL

1807

In 1806 a rumour was circulating that Caroline, Princess of Wales, who had lived with her husband, George, for only three nights in 1795, had since then taken various lovers and given birth to a boy. Caroline had settled in a house in Shooters Hill, South London, where she gave dinners and parties, inviting those who were hostile to her husband, including the Conservative politician George Canning, who was later to become Prime Minister and was allegedly one of her many lovers. Lord Grenville, Prime Minister of the short-lived Whig administration – The Broad Bottomed Ministry (1806–7) – was forced to clear the air and set up an inquiry to examine the allegations. The inquiry, known as the Delicate Investigation, found that Caroline was guilty of unbecoming conduct by flirting with a number of unmarried men, but it cleared her of bearing a son. Spencer Perceval, who had briefly been the Attorney General in William Pitt's last Tory administration before the Whig government, as a leading opposition figure and a devout evangelical Christian now decided to take up the case of Caroline on the grounds that she had been badly treated by her profligate and libertine husband (later George IV).

With the help of Caroline, Perceval compiled a pamphlet known as 'The Book', which exonerated the Princess, cast blame on the

Prince and listed his adulterous liaisons. Perceval even went as far as having 1,500–2,000 of these pamphlets printed, storing them in his house and threatening to sell them unless the Princess's actions were overlooked and King George III ended her exclusion from the court. The Prince of Wales furiously declared that he felt he 'could jump on Perceval and stamp out his life with his feet'. By January 1807 the King had second thoughts and allowed the Princess to return to court circles.

So Perceval's campaign to support Caroline triumphed, but ten days later the Whig government fell over the issue of Catholic emancipation. George III commanded Pitt's friends, including Perceval, to form a new government. Perceval recognised that the publication of 'The Book', which threw a lurid light on the activities of the Prince of Wales, could be a huge embarrassment and so he burnt as many copies as he could in a bonfire in Lincoln's Inn Fields. But not all the copies were destroyed, for Perceval had lent one copy to each of the former Whig Cabinet Ministers and to several of his friends. The printer, Richard Edwards, had also sent out some free copies. So the Treasury solicitor, together with the Prince of Wales's secretary, McMahon, offered payments for returned copies. William Cobbett, the radical writer and journalist, reported that £3,300 was spent on buying back just five copies. Thus what might have been intended as an instrument to destroy a Whig government became something that had to be destroyed to save a Tory government. Perceval may well have kept a copy of 'The Book' himself, realising its value in any future dealings with the Prince of Wales, and later the Prince believed that following Perceval's assassination in 1812 a copy was stolen from No.10 Downing Street.

In 1809 the aged Tory Prime Minister, the Duke of Portland, had a stroke and George III appointed Spencer Perceval as his Prime Minister over the stronger claims of Lord Hawkesbury (later Lord Liverpool) and George Canning: both were later to become prime ministers. George was clearly attracted by Perceval's evangelical Protestantism and his utter hostility to the Catholic Church.

In 1810 George III succumbed to his final bout of insanity and the Prince of Wales assumed the powers of the monarchy as Regent.

In January 1811 London was awash with rumours that Perceval would be sacked and a new prime minister would be appointed by the Prince of Wales from among his old Whig friends. At White's Club the betting was on the Regent's sacking Perceval – on the west wall of Temple Bar someone had scrawled 'The Prince and No Perceval'. But in February the Whig leaders fell out among themselves and the solid country Tory MPs rallied to Perceval. George, without much enthusiasm, confirmed him in office. Britain was at war and actually on the retreat in the Spanish Peninsula, so a change of government would have added to the crisis – the City of London spoke for Britain when bank stocks rose by eight per cent as the news spread that there would be no change.

Cobbett believed that Perceval stayed in office only by blackmailing the Regent over 'The Book'. George Cruikshank, then the leading cartoonist, depicted the Prince of Wales as a huge whale which had been harpooned by Perceval. The harpoon had the words 'Delicate Inquiry' on it – implying that Perceval had a hold over the King as a result of the inquiry he had conducted in 1806. However, Perceval never needed to exercise this pressure – indeed, it was not in his nature to be so devious. Moreover in 1813, Lady Douglas, who had been the prime accuser in 1806, revived the rumour of an illegitimate son and the House of Commons re-examined the Delicate Investigation. At least some copies of 'The Book' survived, since the Whigs, still out of office, seized upon it and published it.

Spencer Perceval, is standing in the boat having hooked the Regent with a harpoon bearing the inscription 'Delicate Inquiry'. All that The Whig Sheridan, on the left, gets a spout of water. Cartoon by Cruikshank, 1812.

THE ROYAL SCANDAL

1809

In January 1809 Colonel Wardle MP, disgruntled about his lack of promotion, attacked in the House of Commons the Duke of York, George III's second son and Commander-in-Chief of the British Army. The grounds were that the Duke's mistress, Mrs Clarke, had made money selling promotions in the Army – appointments to be ensigns, captains or majors – and that some of this money had been given to the Duke to settle his debts. The scandal dominated the press and caricature prints for several months.

In February the House of Commons set up an inquiry, which only made matters worse. Mrs Clarke appeared as a witness on several days and reported that she had 'pinned up a list of names for promotion at the head of my bed and HRH took it down'. It also emerged that she had tried to obtain a bishopric for a certain Dr O'Meara. The inquiry exonerated the Duke but on the following day,

The burning of the Clarke book.

BURNING BY CONTRACT or the fate of the Loves of FREDERICK AND MARY ANN.

to the chagrin of his father, he resigned as Commander-in-Chief. He was later to be reinstated as by his brother, the Prince of Wales, when the latter became Regent in 1811.

As Mrs Clarke had got nothing from the Parliamentary proceedings she decided to publish an account of her life including letters from the Duke. She found a publisher, Sir Richard Phillips (a radical who had been imprisoned for eighteen months in 1793 for publishing Tom Paine's *Rights of Man*), and a printer, Mr Gillett, and they advertised her book. The government, led by the Prime Minister, Perceval, and the Crown decided to prevent the book's publication by offering Mrs Clarke the sum of £10,000 and an annuity for her daughters of £400 a year. An agreement was drawn up which stipulated that the Duke's letters to her should be burnt: 'Conditions to be observed: Mrs Clarke shall give up her *Life* to be consumed by fire, that she shall burn the Manuscript and all the love letters.'

In this print Mrs Clarke is consigning her letters to the flames while the Duke urges her on to 'burn away, burn away'. Perceval, wearing a wig, asks Phillips, the publisher, to swear on the Bible that there is 'not one sheet remaining' but papers are sticking out of Phillips's back pocket bearing the heading 'A Few Sheets of Mrs Clarke's *Life* for private use'. One copy of the *Life* survived and was deposited in Drummond's Bank; it is now in the Public Record Office.

Queen Charlotte. *After Johann Zoffany c. 1775.*

QUEEN CHARLOTTE (1744–1818)

1818

When his mother, Queen Charlotte, died in 1818 the Prince Regent distributed many of her possessions around the family and what was left was sent to public auction. His sisters, who had lived with their mother in Windsor for most of their lives, managed to hang on to their jewellery, resisting George's decree that it all belonged to the State as Crown Jewels. The only thing they all agreed on was that the Queen's

Sales by auction! — or Provident Children disposing of their deceased Mother's Effects for the Benefit of the Creditors !!

Cartoon by George Cruickshank 1819.

instructions for her papers to be burnt should be followed. The executors announced that 'of the papers all that were material have been destroyed including, with their Royal Highnesses' permission, the letters from the Princesses'. Major secrets went up in flames – the obscene behaviour of George III in his illnesses; Princess Amelia's passion for General Fitzroy; and whether the father of Princess Sophia's illegitimate son was her own brother, the Duke of Cumberland – alas, all the evidence was burnt.

The sale of the Queen's goods actually took place at Christie's. Here, George, the Regent, is depicted as the auctioneer, ensuring that the proceeds did not go to the State, but remained with the royal family.

KING GEORGE IV (1762–1830)

1830

After George IV died in 1830 his Private Secretary, Sir William Knighton, and the Duke of Wellington were very concerned about the existence of letters that had passed between George and Maria Fitzherbert.

In 1784 George, at the age of twenty-three, had fallen madly in love with Maria Fitzherbert, a beautiful Catholic who had already been twice widowed. She eventually succumbed to George's passionate wooing – some of his letters to her were over twenty pages long – and became his mistress. On 15 December 1785 in her drawing room in Park Street the couple were married by an Anglican clergyman, who risked hanging, as it was a capital offence for anyone to officiate at the marriage of the heir to the throne without the approval of the King. The marriage, however, was invalid, since the Royal Marriages Act of 1772 required the Prince to obtain from his father, King George III, his approval, which was not sought and certainly would not have been given. Furthermore the Act of Settlement of 1701 excluded from the throne anyone who married a papist. However,

Left: Maria Fitzherbert *by Sir Joshua Reynolds, c. 1788.*

Right: George IV while Prince Regent *by Sir Thomas Lawrence, c. 1814.*

Gillray depicts the scandalous marriage of the Prince of Wales to the twice-widowed Roman Catholic Maria Fitzherbert. Charles James Fox is the best man and Edmund Burke is the priest, while the Prime Minister, North, falls asleep. A marriage ceremony did in fact take place in Maria's drawing room in Park Street, Mayfair, on 15 December 1785.

the Catholic Church held that the marriage had taken place. This relationship lasted for over twenty-four years, although during that time George took other mistresses, but they did not last very long. The marriage to Maria finally came to an end in 1811. George gave her an annuity of £6,000 a year, to be increased on his death to £10,000. The pair maintained a reasonably friendly relationship. After George died in 1830 Wellington found a locket around his neck containing a miniature of her.

There was much speculation as to whether George and Maria had had a child and some prints showed her holding a baby. Towards the end of her life she prepared a document which stated, 'I, Maria Fitzherbert, moreover testify that my union with George, Prince of Wales, was without issue.' Somewhat enigmatically, she did not sign it in the place provided.

There were prolonged negotiations over George's letters and a formal agreement was drawn up in August 1833, as Maria Fitzherbert had intended to publish both her letters to George and those from him as a vindication after her death. Wellington was alarmed and wanted

WIFE & no WIFE __ or __ A trip to the Continent,

all the letters destroyed. Maria was allowed to keep the essential letters which included the mortgage on the Pavilion, the marriage certificate, the Will of 1796, a letter written by Robert Burt – the clergyman who had married the couple – and the Prince's long letter of 1785. Others were handed over in the drawing room of Tilney Street to Wellington and Maria's representative, Lord Albemarle, where they were burnt. So many had to be consigned to the flames that Wellington remarked, after some hours, 'I think my Lord we had better hold our hand for a while or we shall set the old woman's chimney afire.' Thomas Creevey, the Clerk to the Privy Council, lamented in his diary, 'Oh dear, oh dear! That I could have seen them! They began in 1785 and lasted to 1806 when the young man fell in love with Lady Hertford.'

Mrs Arbuthnot, Wellington's mistress, revealed that other letters from George to his last mistress, Lady Conyngham, had also been burnt. Lady Conyngham had been George's companion from 1820 to 1830. Mrs Arbuthnot wrote, 'Volumes of love letters, chiefly from Lady Conyngham, some foul copies of his own to Lady Conyngham descriptive of the most furious passion, trinkets of all sorts, quantities of women's gloves, dirty snuffy pocket handkerchiefs with old faded nosegays tied up in them…. He said he thought the best thing would be to burn them all.'

Sir William Knighton, George IV's Private Secretary, was also in the business of tidying up the King's reputation. He ordered the burning of 'several drawerfuls of freeprints and drawings: the private property of his late Majesty'. This was indeed a great sadness, for George had kept many caricatures in which he was the victim.

A large number of letters must have survived, for one evening in 1913 George V, Queen Mary and their Private Secretary sat in a parlour in Windsor and systematically burnt the contents of thirty-seven boxes of George IV's love letters, including many to Mrs Fitzherbert. Their grounds were that George was 'the meanest and vilest of reprobates'.

THE MUNSHI

1887–1901

To celebrate her Golden Jubilee in 1887 Queen Victoria decided to have two Indian servants to underline her position as Empress of India. One of those recommended was Abdul Karim, a twenty-four-year-old Muslim from Agra. He was reasonably well educated, being able to speak Persian as well as Hindustani, and had come to the attention of the Director of Prisons in Agra as he had helped him to parcel up Indian carpets made by prisoners and sent to England. Karim was therefore considered trustworthy, a good servant, and to his great advantage he was a handsome, imposing young man. He was given lessons in English, etiquette and history before leaving for Windsor.

Queen Victoria and the Munshi, photograph, c. 1894.

Karim attended upon Queen Victoria during the Jubilee celebrations, establishing himself at the court where he and his wife

won some popularity by preparing curries, which caught the attention and the appetite of the Queen. He moved with her to Osborne, on the Isle of Wight, where she asked him to give her lessons in Hindustani – becoming in effect her teacher, the 'Munshi'. This established a relationship that was quite different from that with her other servants and she became so fluent in Hindustani that she was able to keep a daily record in it.

Victoria appointed Karim as her Secretary and his first task was to stand beside her to blot her signature. This led to him ordering her papers and making copies at her request – she told her daughter Vicky, 'he looks after all my boxes'. This meant that he saw many confidential minutes concerning not only affairs of State, but also letters about her extended family across Europe. This privileged and unique role was resented by the circle of courtiers around the Queen, who were appalled when Karim was allowed a carriage of his own with a footman and given John Brown's old room. Victoria wrote him many letters, signing herself 'Your Dearest Friend', or 'Your True Friend' and even 'Your Dearest Mother' and she gave him various honours, making him a member of the Victorian Order and, at a much higher level, a Companion of the Indian Empire. At her Diamond Jubilee Victoria even considered making him a Knight of the Indian Empire. Her Private Secretary and her doctor, who was in daily attendance, could not stand for this and the Prime Minister, Lord Salisbury, had to be called in to kill off the idea on the grounds that such an honour to a Muslim would offend the Hindus. They were also concerned that Karim could be a spy: did he have friends who were secretly undermining the Imperial government of India? Each Viceroy was asked to investigate, but no evidence of treachery was found. Each Viceroy also had to get used to receiving letters from the Queen about Indian matters which could have been gleaned only from what the Munshi had told her.

Victoria robustly defended Karim and ordered the Viceroy to make a grant of land in Agra to him as a reward for his services. The Colonial Service at first baulked at this, but they had not counted upon Victoria's relentless stubbornness and eventually the Munshi was granted the land, which was to make him a rich man. The hostility towards him was not political: it was racist and snobbish.

The courtiers around the Queen did not want to eat with a man who in India would have been treated as a menial servant.

Victoria died at Osborne House on 22 January 1901. The last person to see her before the coffin was sealed was the Munshi. Victoria had decreed before her death that at her funeral Karim was to be included in the group of personal mourners, something which the household would never have allowed. Almost immediately after her death Edward VII sent his sister, Princess Beatrice, Victoria's youngest daughter, and his wife, Queen Alexandra, to Frogmore Cottage, the Munshi's house at Windsor, to seize all Victoria's letters to the Munshi. When these had been collected, from an astonished and tearful family, they were burnt in a fire outside the house. Abdul Karim was told that as his services were no longer required, he could pack his bags and return to India.

Edward VII continued to be worried about what could emerge from the relationship between his mother and her servant, which he had always opposed. In April 1909, when Edward heard of the Munshi's death in Agra, he ordered the Viceroy 'to ensure that any existing letters of the Munshi Abdul Karim … do not fall into improper hands'. Only a handful of harmless letters were found, but nonetheless most were destroyed.

In 2011 a frail, elderly and blind lady, Begum Qamar Jehan, gave to the author of a book on the Munshi some letters and his diary, which she, being a distant relative, had held in safekeeping. The diary told of Karim's life, 'As I have been but a sojourner in a strange land and among a strange people', and it reveals a devoted servant who loved the Queen, taught her Hindustani, was with her on her travels and almost constantly at her side. The fretful courtiers around the Queen had no reason to be anxious. There were no indiscretions, harmful comments or unfavourable descriptions of Victoria's family or friends. Karim knew the courtiers did not like him and he went as far as saying one year, 'The unpleasantness I remarked on last year still existed.' The bonfire in 1901 had not been needed.

LUCKY
ESCAPES

PUBLIUS VERGILIUS MARO (VIRGIL, 70–19BC)

Saving the *Aeneid*

Virgil was the pre-eminent poet in the Augustan age of Rome. He was encouraged by the Emperor himself and spent seven years writing the *Aeneid*. It was to become one of the founding myths of ancient Rome, for it tells of the journey that Aeneas took after the fall of Troy to Carthage and then Italy, where he is depicted as one of the founders of the city.

Legend has it that around 19BC Virgil travelled to Greece. After seeing Augustus in Athens he returned to Rome, but succumbed to a fever that led to his death in the port of Brundisium. At that stage the *Aeneid* was not complete and Virgil left a wish that it should be

Virgil, mosaic,
Roman,
third century AD.

burnt after his death. Augustus countermanded this and instructed the two executors, Lucius Varius Rufus and Plotius Tucca, to publish the *Aeneid* as it stood.

There has been much speculation as to why Virgil wanted his manuscript, which ran to twelve chapters and parts of which he had read to his circle of friends, to be destroyed. There were several half-complete lines and in a search for perfection Virgil may have wanted to finish them. There may have been errors, infelicities, a wrong emphasis – one scholar even argued that as the ending is abrupt and dramatic Virgil intended to write an epilogue. A great deal of meticulous scholarship and exegesis has been devoted to this problem, notably in Sir John Sparrow's paper on *The Incomplete Lines of the Aeneid*, published in 1931.

This is the sort of debate that is unlikely to be resolved, but it was indeed fortunate that Virgil's last wishes were disregarded, otherwise we would have been deprived of one of the greatest poetical works from the classical world.

GEORGE HERBERT (1593–1633)

Born in 1593 of a large family which today would be called upper middle-class, George Herbert went to Cambridge at the age of sixteen and by the age of twenty had become the University's public orator. He was well placed for a career in public life, but when two of his most important patrons died he decided to choose the Church, which was probably his first love. He became the Vicar of St Andrew's, Bemerton, in Wiltshire.

From the age of seven Herbert had been writing poems but none were to be published during his lifetime. He suffered from ill-health and died at the age of thirty-nine in March 1633. When he was dying he sent his handwritten book of poems to his friend Nicholas Ferrar, the founder of the religious community at Little Gidding. His message to Ferrar was: 'If he think it may turn to the advantage of any dejected poor soul, let it be made public; if not, let him burn it.'

Ferrar arranged for the book, which he titled *The Temple*, to be published by the end of 1633. Thus was saved a collection of some of the most beautiful religious and spiritual poems in the English language.

The Temple was an immediate success – four editions were published in three years and it became a favourite of Charles I.

Stained-glass window of George Herbert and Nicholas Ferrar, in Bemerton Church.

THOMAS CARLYLE (1795–1881)

Thomas Carlyle, the great Victorian historian and prophet, died in 1881. In 1882 J.A. Froude, who had over the years become Carlyle's closest friend, was appointed his official biographer. Froude published the first two volumes of his biography, which covered the first forty years of Carlyle's life. These were followed by another two volumes in 1884 which were a history of Carlyle's life in London. In 1871 Carlyle had turned to Froude to write his posthumous biography and in that year he gave Froude a large collection of his private papers: 'These are yours to publish or not to publish as you please after I am gone ... I must publish it, the whole, or else destroy.' Sending him more papers, Carlyle said, "All I can say to you is 'burn freely'".

Carlyle was, in effect, trusting his reputational legacy to his closest friend. When Froude read the papers he discovered very quickly how painful the marriage with Jane Carlyle had been. She had died suddenly, collapsing in a London street when Carlyle was in the North, and he was overwhelmed with remorse at the way he had treated her. The papers Froude had received, including Jane Carlyle's letters, revealed Carlyle's violent outbursts of anger, his refusal to have any children – indeed, the marriage was probably unconsummated – and his infatuation, almost to the extent of grovelling before her, with Lady Ashburton. Jane Carlyle, expecting her marriage to be normal and to have children, was almost driven to suicide.

Froude had to decide whether all this should be revealed. He was puzzled at the way Carlyle had left the decision up to him, but Carlyle had done that at a time when he had stopped writing, his great prophetic reputation was declining and possibly he realised that if Froude did not reflect the fullness of his life, the memory of him would be eroded. What was more likely was that Carlyle realised how very badly he had behaved through his astonishing selfishness and he wanted his friend to record a posthumous atonement.

Froude was a scrupulous historian and believed very strongly in moral integrity. So he published a full warts-and-all biography, but was plagued for much of the rest of his life by friends of Carlyle who reproached him for his frankness. This was not so much a lucky escape as an unlucky one for Carlyle.

Thomas Carlyle
by Carlo
Pellegrini
chromo-
lithograph,
published in
Vanity Fair,
October 1870.

THOMAS HARDY (1840–1928)

Hardy had the habit of destroying the working copies of his poems as soon as he had settled on the final version, of which he had made a copy for the printer – over 900 of these have survived, but only a handful of working drafts.

The amended draft of this poem, 'A Singer Asleep', his elegy on the death of Swinburne, did survive. Hardy admired Swinburne and they became friends and kindred spirits, linked by public contumely – 'we laughed and condoled with each other as having been the two most abused of living writers – he for 'Poems and Ballads' and I for 'Jude the Obscure'.'

'A Singer Asleep', manuscript by Thomas Hardy (from a Sotheby's catalogue).

Swinburne's death in April 1909 was a great shock and Hardy was so appalled by the hypocritical obituaries that he penned this tribute. The changes in his revised draft are quite material. The title is changed and in a characteristic Hardyesque way 'the sleepless sea' was changed to 'the unslumbering sea'.

The fine copy of this poem was given by Sydney Cockerell, Hardy's literary executor, to the Newnes Public Library in Putney, no doubt in recognition of Swinburne's home at No.2 The Pines on Putney Hill. It now rests in the local history library in Battersea.

This poem clearly meant much to Hardy, for he retained this working draft, which his widow, Florence, gave to a friend in 1937. It was later sold at Sotheby's in 2001 and later by a bookseller in 2011 for £21,000.

GERARD MANLEY HOPKINS (1844–1889)

1868

Like Cardinal Newman and Cardinal Manning, Gerard Manley Hopkins started as an Anglican, becoming a Catholic after his studies at Oxford at the age of twenty-two. He was received into the Church by John Newman himself and in the same year he pledged to give up poetry for Lent. Two years later, in May 1868, he decided to become a Jesuit priest and entered his novitiate and less than a week later he made a bonfire of all his poems, resolving 'to write no more, as not belonging to my profession, unless it were by the wish of my superiors'. He called this 'the slaughter of the innocents', but he did have the good sense to send copies of some of these poems to an old friend from his Oxford days, Robert Bridges. Bridges was to become the Poet Laureate but he also became over the years the recipient of Hopkins's poems and without him they would not have survived: he published them in 1918.

During Hopkins's studies and meditation he came across the works of Dun Scotus and his principle of the individual being related to every natural thing. This provided a bridge to Hopkins's own theory of 'inscape', which allowed him to be 'flush with a new enthusiasm. It may come to nothing and it may be a mercy from God but just then when I took in any inscape of the sky or the sea I thought of Scotus.'

Hopkins's seven-year-long denial of poetry ended in 1875 when one of his superiors asked him to write a poem about the sinking of a German ship in which five Franciscan nuns had perished. This led to *The Wreck of the Deutschland*, but his Jesuit superiors declined to print it. Hopkins was ordained in 1877 and in that year he wrote some of his most celebrated poems, *God's Grandeur*, *The Caged Skylark*, *The Windhover*, *Pied Beauty* and *Hurrahing in Harvest*.

The Jesuits looked upon Hopkins as an eccentric, awkward and ineffective teacher and priest. They did not realise they had a genius among them. He was moved to eleven postings in over four counties

Gerard Manley Hopkins.

over eight years, including such towns as Sheffield, Liverpool, Glasgow, towns in industrial Lancashire and finally Dublin, which Hopkins described as 'dank as ditch water'. There was no understanding that here was a man who loved the landscape of the country and all living things in nature that could affect an individual and who coined a new word to describe this experience – 'inscape'.

R.L. STEVENSON (1850–1894)

This is an extract from a letter sent by Robert Louis Stevenson to his closest friend in England, Sidney Colvin, on 30 April 1890, as he was travelling on a boat, S.S. *Janet Nicoll*, from Samoa to Sydney.

> After a day in Auckland, we set sail again; were blown up in the main cabin with calcium fires, as we left the bay: Let no man say I am unscientific; when I ran, on the alert, out of my stateroom and found the main cabin encarnadined with the glow of the last scene of a pantomime, I stopped dead. 'What is this?' said I. 'This ship is on fire. I see that; but why a pantomime?' And I stood and reasoned the point, until my head was so muddled with the fumes that I could

The Stevenson household at Vailima, Samoa, 1892 (RLS sits centre-back row with Fanny beside him).

not find the companion. A few seconds later, the captain had to enter crawling on his belly and took days to recover (if he has recovered) from the fumes. By singular good fortune, we got the hose down in time and saved the ship, but Lloyd lost most of his clothes and a great part of our photographs was destroyed. Fanny saw the native sailors tossing overboard a blazing trunk; she stopped them in time and behold! it contained my manuscripts.

The fire had been caused by one of Stevenson's fellow travellers bringing on board some fireworks (including ten pounds of 'calcium fire' with fumes) for the entertainment of his native retainers in Auckland. On 20 April just as they were leaving Auckland Harbour the fireworks exploded and almost caused the ship to be lost. Stevenson was then working on the final chapters of *The Wreckers*, a novel he was writing with his stepson, Lloyd Osbourne; his collection of South Sea poems, some of which were later published in *Songs of Travel*; the outline of a novel – *The Pearl Fishers* – which he never got around to finishing or even starting; and a series of essays on his travels from San Francisco to Honolulu and south through the Islands, which were published after his death as *In the South Seas*. Much of this material was in the trunk, saved by Fanny Stevenson.

FRANZ KAFKA (1883–1924)

In 1921 Franz Kafka had told his oldest and most devoted friend, Max Brod, 'My will is going to be quite simple – a request to you to burn everything.' In 1923 Kafka, together with his lover, Dora Diamond, had burnt a large amount of material including a short story, *The Burrow*, a play and a story about a ritual murder in Odessa. He said he had burnt them to keep warm.

Kafka suffered from tuberculosis and knew he could die at almost any time. He wrote an undated letter to Max Brod which was found in his writing desk.

Dearest Max

My last wish: everything I leave behind in the way of diaries, manuscripts, letters of my own and from others, drawings, etc. ... should be burned, completely and unread, as should everything written or drawn in your possession or the possession of others, whom you should ask in my name, to do likewise. People who do not want to hand over letters to you should at least be made to promise that they themselves will burn them.
Yours

Franz Kafka, 1906.

Franz Kafka

That was clear enough and it was reinforced by another letter to Brod, written in pencil, dated 29 November, possibly in the year 1922. However, some scholars have argued that Kafka did not mean a word of it as he knew that Brod would not do it, and Brod later said he had actually told Kafka he would not. So why did Kafka, who was a lawyer and fully aware of legally enforceable agreements, not leave instructions to destroy his papers, if he really meant that, in other hands?

In any event, none of this mattered, for Brod decided to print what Kafka had left. Before his death in 1924 Kafka had published only one important novel – *Metamorphosis* – and some lesser works – *Judgement, Stoker, Penal Colony, Country Doctor.* So it fell to Brod to arrange the printing of Kafka's two masterpieces, *The Trial* (1925) and *The Castle* (1926). *Amerika* (1927), *The Great Wall of China and other stories* (1931) and Kafka's diaries of 1910–23 also appeared after his death.

In 1939, the night before the Nazis invaded Prague, Brod fled to Tel Aviv with two suitcases filled with Kafka's letters and manuscripts. Later depositing them in a bank in Switzerland, in 1961 Brod gave them to the Bodleian Library, which had become a leading centre for Kafka's textual research. The only manuscript Brod retained was *The Trial*, which he considered as a personal gift, and after his death it passed to his secretary, Esther Hoffe. The manuscript was later sold at Sotheby's for £1.1 million.

KATHERINE MANSFIELD (1893–1923)

Before she died at the early age of thirty-four from pneumonia, aggravated by undiagnosed gonorrhoea, Katherine Mansfield had published three volumes of short stories which had brought her literary recognition and some fame. She had also for eight years confided her thoughts about the people she met, her relationships – not only with her husband – and her ambitions to a Journal. She had asked her husband, John Middleton Murry, to 'tear up and burn as much as possible … destroy all letters you do not wish to keep…. Have a clean sweep, Bogey, and leave all fair – will you?' Her literary estate was vast: the Journal, letters, a scrapbook and enough short stories for Murry to publish two further volumes.

Murry's own writings are now forgotten but he lives on through an act of resurrection of his wife's work. He was heartily hated by several contemporaries – 'the best hated man of letters'; 'the man who made Mansfield miserable'; and Virginia Woolf, some of whose essays he published in *The Athenaeum*, was blunter, 'the one vile man I have ever known'.

Katherine Mansfield *by Anne Estelle Rice, 1918.*

Murry disregarded his wife's wishes, publishing a heavily edited and sanitised version of her work which depicted her in a saintly way, leading one of her biographers to conclude that 'he sealed her in porcelain'. After Murry's death in 1957 various scholars, using the letters that survived, were able to depict Mansfield's extraordinary talents and passionate sensuality in a more realistic and human way.

C.S. LEWIS (1898–1963)

Shortly after C.S. Lewis's death his brother, Major Warren Lewis, destroyed many of his papers on a bonfire 'which burned steadily for three days'. He also instructed the gardener to burn some of his brother's notebooks, but the gardener pleaded that they should be left until they were seen by Walter Hooper, who was a friend of the writer and an Anglican priest and

C.S. Lewis Hoax jacket.

who had worked for a time as his secretary. Hooper discovered two sets of manuscripts – a long fragment of a novel, *The Dark Tower*, which he published in 1977, and a collection of children's stories, *Boxen*, published in 1985. Lewis had apparently written *Boxen* when he was only six or seven years old.

In 1988 a Lewis scholar, Kathryn Lindskoog, from Redlands, California, wrote a book entitled *The C.S. Lewis Hoax* which was published by the Multinomah School of the Bible in Portland, Oregon. It alleged that the two books were a confidence trick by Hooper and his friend Anthony Marchington. However, neither had profited from the publications. This remarkable charge arose from the fact that Lindskoog and Hooper were both fanatical admirers of Lewis, but also rivals. Hooper had written Lewis's biography and Lindskoog boasted that the great man had said to her in a letter that she understood his work better than anyone else.

In 1989 a panel of four Oxford dons was asked by the C.S. Lewis Foundation of Christian High Education in Redlands to resolve the dispute. Unanimously they found that the two books were genuine and one of the dons, Dr Judith Priestman, said, 'It is terrible that such accusations were made.' Lindskoog dismissed the findings, although she had never seen the manuscripts, but Hooper, not surprisingly, was delighted: 'I have been terribly hurt by these awful allegations. At times I have wanted to go to sleep and just not wake up.'

Hooper also came to realise that scattered through the notebooks was Lewis's translation of the *Aeneid*, the existence of which was known, since Tolkien remembered him reading it at a meeting of their literary discussion group, The Inklings, of which they were members. To put the translation together had been a demanding task of scholarship and a real labour of love: it was not completed (by A.T. Reyes) until 2011, when it was published by Yale University Press.

VLADIMIR NABOKOV (1899–1977)

Nabokov was working on his final novel, *Laura*, when he died. He must have been aware he had only a short time left as he had suffered from a series of falls, hospital infections and congestive bronchitis. Like *Edwin Drood* the novel was not finished and Nabokov gave explicit instructions to his wife, Vera, to destroy the incomplete manuscript. However, she did not and it remained locked in a Swiss bank vault. A handful of people had seen it and declared it to be a masterpiece. Nabokov's son, Dimitri, who had inherited the obligation, considered it to 'have been Father's most brilliant novel'. Nabokov had once before used the incinerator, but Vera had prevented her husband from committing an early version of *Lolita* to the flames.

Dimitri struggled with his conscience for over thirty years and then explained why he gave in:

Nabokov and his wife Vera.

I have said and written more than once that to me my parents, in a sense, had never died but lived on, looking over my shoulder in a kind of virtual limbo, able to offer a thought or counsel in order to assist me in a vital decision, were it a crucial *mot juste* or some more mundane concern. If it pleases an imaginative commentator to liken the case to mystical phenomena, so be it.

So the blame for *Laura*'s survival fell on his ghostly parents.

Dimitri, obeying the voices of his parents from the grave, allowed Penguin to publish this supposedly great novel in 2009. It was written in pencil with very clear writing on 138 small index cards and Penguin published the book in such a way that each perforated index card could be taken out. Critical acclaim was muted. At best it was the outline of a short story. Martin Amis, who admires Nabokov as one of the great stylists of the twentieth century, commented: 'This relic is the slight exacerbation of what is already a problem from Hell … *Laura* joins *The Enchanter* (1939), *Lolita* (1955), *Ada* (1970), *Transparent Things* (1972) and *Look at the Harlequins* (1974) in unignorably concerning itself with the sexual despoliation of very young girls…'. Other contemporary writers were divided: Tom Stoppard said 'burn it'; John Banville 'save it'.

The critical reaction showed that Dimitri's claim that the novel was 'an embryonic masterpiece' was either a gross misjudgement or a con-trick. One critic dismissed it as 'an elegant literary folly'; another that it 'may have inflicted some severe damage on his father's reputation'; another as 'fragments of a novel, not a novel of fragments' and 'it looks like a joker being played from beyond the grave'.

It seems to me that Nabokov knew exactly what he wanted, for in his first English-language novel, *The Real Life of Sebastian Knight*, Sebastian's brother says:

> 'My first duty after Sebastian's death was to go through his belongings. He had left everything to me and I had a letter from him instructing me to burn certain of his papers … but I soon found out that except for a few odd pages dispersed among other papers, he himself had destroyed them long ago, for he belonged to that rare type of writer who knows that nothing ought to remain except for the perfect achievement, the printed book … the litter of the workshop, no matter its sentimental or commercial value, must never subsist.'

In 1962, when Nabokov was asked whether there was a rough draft of *Lolita*, he majestically replied, 'only ambitious non-entities and hearty mediocrities exhibit their rough drafts. It is like passing around samples of one's sputum.'

Dimitri should perhaps have realised that the last card in the book reflected the author's view, for it contained only these words, 'efface, expunge, excise, delete, rub out, wipe out, obliterate'.

DYLAN THOMAS (1914–1953)

Dylan Thomas,
illustration by Dan Peterson.

Dylan Thomas lost the manuscript of *Under Milk Wood* three times: first in London, then in America and once again in London.

The mid-Thirties were one of the most prolific creative periods for Thomas: his first book, *Eighteen Poems*, was published in 1934 and his second collection, *Twenty-Five Poems,* in 1936. In a letter to a friend in 1935 he explained the process of his composition:

> 'My method is this: I write a poem on innumerable sheets of scrap paper, write it on both sides of the paper, often upside down and criss-cross ways unpunctuated, surrounded by drawings of lampposts and boiled eggs in a very dirty mess; bit by bit I copy out the slowly developing poem into an exercise book; and, when it is completed, I type it out. The scrap sheets I burn.'

Thomas said later that he had 'about ten exercise books full of poems'. Four of these are in the State University of Buffalo, but another emerged in 2014 which appeared to be a follow-on to these four. It was discarded between 1936, when the poems were published, and 1941, when he sold the four. The notebook that emerged in 2014 had been left in the house of Thomas's mother-in-law, Mary MacNamara, in Blashford, Hampshire, where he stayed frequently towards the end of the 1930s. The notebook was given to Louie King, who worked in the house, to be burnt. Before she died in 1984 she had added a short note saying, 'This book of poetry by Dylan Thomas was with a lot of papers given to me to burn in the kitchen boiler. I saved it and forgot all about it until I read of his death.' The King family decided to sell the notebook in December 2014 at Sotheby's, where it realised £85,000. I am indebted to the scrupulous scholarship of the cataloguer. This book contains nineteen poems amended and rewritten, including several variants from the text that was published. It includes the sonnet sequence *Alterwise by owl-light*, which was one of Dylan Thomas's most challenging poems.

Dylan Thomas manuscript.

Julia Brown, who has been helping me with the illustrations for this book, told me of an extraordinary episode of how some of her family's archive was saved because of 'Totter's Rights' – something that has been discarded as rubbish, i.e. on a skip, can be legally taken by someone who has found it. 'Tot' may originate from the German for 'dead'.

TOTTER'S RIGHTS

(Darcy Braddell 1884-1970) (Dorothy Braddell 1889-1981)

Several years after the architect Darcy Braddell had died in 1970 his wife sorted through his papers and threw away a shoebox of letters from him to her and from their various and interesting friends to him. He was a keen letter writer and they had a wide circle of friends in the literary and architectural worlds (A.P. Herbert, Paul and John Nash, Byam Shaw, Edwin Lutyens, etc), and their house in Holland Park was much visited.

The shoebox, unknown to any of the family, was put in the dustbin by my grandmother in a typically methodical and careful clear out before her death about a year later. Two years after that I was told that a collection of letters to and from Darcy Braddell were in the catalogue of an antiquarian book dealer in Kensington, with a fairly substantial price tag. The family were surprised and rather disturbed that private correspondence had resurfaced, and sent me to investigate. Apparently as dustmen have 'Totter's Rights' so one had legitimately sold an old shoe box of letters to the book dealer. We paid up (apparently we were in competition with the Huntington Library) respecting my grandmother's wishes, and the letters are now back, undisturbed, in the family archive. The moral of this (pre-shredding) story is that if you want to destroy paper you really must burn it!

JULIA BROWN

EPILOGUE

And yet the books will be there on the shelves, separate beings,
That appeared once, still wet
As shining chestnuts under a tree in autumn,
And, touched, coddled, began to live
In spite of fires on the horizon, castles blown up,
Tribes on the march, planets in motion,
'We are,' they said, even as their pages
Were being torn out, or a buzzing flame
Licked away their letters. So much more durable
Than we are, whose frail warmth
Cools down with memory, disperses, perishes.
I imagine the earth when I am no more:
Nothing happens, no loss, it's still a strange pageant,
Women's dresses, dewy lilacs, a song in the valley.
Yet the books will be there on the shelves, well born,
Derived from people, but also from radiance, heights.

CZESLAW MILOSZ (1911–2004)
Translated by Czeslaw Milosz and Robert Hass

DON'T THINK IT WILL GET BETTER IN THE FUTURE

Salman Rushdie

In March 2016, it was reported that forty-two state-run media outlets in Iran had pooled together to raise $600,000 to add to the fatwa on Salman Rushdie – twenty-seven years after the Ayatollah called for his assassination. In 1998 Iran's former President Mohammad Khatami said the fatwa was 'finished', but the clerical leaders never give up.

China

In March 2016 Beijing muzzled its most famous and determined critic Ren Zhiqiang – the former soldier and property tycoon who had retired in 2014. The Cyberspace Administration of China – the word 'inquisition' would have sufficed – closed down his social media account, the equivalent of Twitter, that had 38 million followers – for spreading 'illegal information that had caused a bad impact'. Zhiqiang had dared to criticise the Communist Party's grip on state media.

Xi Jinping the President, speaking to the leading party controlled media organisations declared that it was their duty to focus on 'positive reporting', 'speak for the Party's will' and 'protect the Party's authority and unity'. One senior journalist who withheld his name said, 'Now all that is left is political propaganda on the one hand, or entertainment and public relations on the other'.

Back to the future.

Matthew Evans, the former Chairman of Faber and
Faber, had been appointed the Chairman of the
Library and Information Commission and in 1997
he published a report, *New Library – The People's
Network*. Having worked closely with Ted Hughes in
his Faber days, Matthew asked him to write a poem
for the report, and I asked Ted to sign a copy of the
final draft over lunch at the Groucho Club. This
great poem is about the importance of libraries but
appears to have dropped through all the records of
his works as it is not in his collected poems, nor in his
bibliography.

For Kenneth and Mary all the very best as always

Ted

August 1998

HEAR IT AGAIN

'For out of olde feldes, as men seyth,
Cometh al this newe corne yer by yere,
And out of old bokes, in good feyth,
Cometh al this newe science that men lere.'
Chaucer: *The Parlement of Foules*

Fourteen centuries have learned,
From charred remains, that what took place
When Alexandria's library burned
Brain-damaged the human race.

Whatever escaped
Was hidden by bookish monks in their damp cells
Hunted by Alfred dug for by Charlemagne
Got through the Dark Ages little enough but enough
For Dante and Chaucer sitting up all night
looking for light.

A Serbian Prof's insanity,
Commanding guns, to split the heart,
His and his people's, tore apart
The Sarajevo library.

Tyrants know where to aim
As Hitler poured his petrol and tossed matches
Stalin collected the bards----
In other words the mobile and only libraries----
of all those enslaved peoples from the Black to
the Bering Sea.

And made a bonfire
Of the mainspring of national identities to melt
       the folk into one puddle
And the three seconds of the present moment
By massacring those wordy fellows whose memories were
       bigger than armies.

Where any nation starts awake
Books are the memory. And it's plain
Decay of libraries is like
Alzheimer's in the nation's brain.

And in my own day in my own land
I have heard the fiery whisper: 'We are here
To destroy the Book
To destroy the rooted stock of the Book and
The Book's perennial vintage, destroy it
Not with a hammer not with a sickle
And not exactly according to Mao who also
Drained the skull of adult and adolescent
To build a shining new society
With the empties----'

For this one's dreams and that one's acts,
For all who've failed or aged beyond
The reach of teachers, here are found
The inspiration and the facts.

As we all know and have heard all our lives
Just as we've heard that here.

Even the most misfitting child
Who's chanced upon the library's worth,
Sits with the genius of the Earth
And turns the key to the whole world.

Ted

July 1997

PICTURE CREDITS AND ACKNOWLEDGEMENTS

Cover and section openers: shutterstock.com

Internal images: British Library: 20, © The British Library Board. Royal 6. E.VI, f.255; AKG: 25, ©akg-images / Erich Lessing; 55, ©akg-images / ullstein bild; 76, ©akg-images / Zhou Thong/ Lebrecht: 65, Sputnik/Lebrecht Music & Arts; Getty images: 77, AFP Photo/Alessandro Abbonizio/Getty images; 123, Neil Jacobs/Getty Images; 125, AFP Photo/Jaafar Ashtiyeh; 143, Mario Tama/Getty Images/ Bridgeman: 81, British Library, London, UK / © British Library Board. All Rights Reserved / Bridgeman Images; 88, © Glasgow University Library, Scotland / Bridgeman Images; 105, Museum of Art, Tula, Russia / Bridgeman Images; 108, London Metropolitan Archives, City of London / Bridgeman Images; 112, Fitzwilliam Museum, University of Cambridge, UK / Bridgeman Images; 162 and 164, Private Collection / © Look and Learn / Bridgeman Images; 183, Fitzwilliam Museum, University of Cambridge, UK / Bridgeman Images; 187, 193, 197, 236 and 242 Private Collection / Bridgeman Images; 216, © Museum of London, UK / Bridgeman Images; 230, The Illustrated London News Picture Library, London, UK / Bridgeman Images; 246, Museum of New Zealand Te Papa Tongarewa, Wellington, New Zealand / Bridgeman Images © DACS/ Alamy: 91, © North Wind Picture Archives / Alamy Stock Photo 159, © World History Archive / Alamy Stock Photo/ Science Museum: 115, ©Daily Herald Archive/National Media Museum/Science & Society Picture Library/ Press Association: 117, ©AP/Press Association Images/ Reuters: 127, Reuters/Esam AL-Fetori; 145, Reuters/ Mohamed Abd El-Ghany/ Diomedia: 135, © Josse Fine Art / DIOMEDIA /National Portrait Gallery: 162, 172, 180-181 and 241 © National Portrait Gallery, London / Rex Features: 207, Tina Norris / Rex / Shutterstock /Art Achive: 211, The Art Archive / Museo della Civilta Romana Rome / Collection Dagli Orti.

Every effort has been made to trace copyright holders and to obtain their permission for the use of copyright material. The publisher apologises for any errors or omissions in the above list and would be grateful if notified of any corrections that should be incorporated in future reprints or editions of this book.

*A plaque in Römerberg Square, Frankfurt, commemorating the
burning of thousands of books by National Socialist students in Berlin
on 10 May 1933.*

INDEX

HEAR IT AGAIN

'For out of olde feldes, as men seyth,
Cometh al this newe corne yer by yere,
And out of old bokes, in good feyth,
Cometh al this newe science that men lere.'
Chaucer: *The Parlement of Foules*

Fourteen centuries have learned,
From charred remains, that what took place
When Alexandria's library burned
Brain-damaged the human race.

Whatever escaped
Was hidden by bookish monks in their damp cells
Hunted by Alfred dug for by Charlemagne
Got through the Dark Ages little enough but enough
For Dante and Chaucer sitting up all night
looking for light.

A Serbian Prof's insanity,
Commanding guns, to split the heart,
His and his people's, tore apart
The Sarajevo library.

Tyrants know where to aim
As Hitler poured his petrol and tossed matches
Stalin collected the bards----
In other words the mobile and only libraries----
of all those enslaved peoples from the Black to
the Bering Sea.